Access your Online Resources

Unlocking Inclusion for SEN Learners is accompanied by a number of printable online materials, designed to ensure this resource best supports your professional needs.

Go to https://resourcecentre.routledge.com/speechmark and click on the cover of this book

UNLOCKING INCLUSION FOR SEN LEARNERS

Being included in a meaningful and intentional sense is often the key that can unlock access to education, learning and the maximising of potential for many children and young people. However, an increasing number of pupils have a variety of strengths that are only shown when they are intentionally included, and their needs are well met.

This book emphasises the key message that the adaptions we make to our daily practice are crucial for some but helpful for all. It provides the tools to unlock whole-school inclusion and ensure each child is given the opportunity to fulfil their potential. Each chapter:

❖ Provides practical, impactful ideas that are easy and cost-effective to action, designed to help primary schools make active inclusion a reality.

❖ Explores the development of a dynamic, evolving whole school inclusive ethos and environment that is responsive to SEN needs.

❖ Considers how we create inclusive classrooms through environmental design and adaptive high-quality teaching.

❖ Is broken down into clear areas of SEN support and contains a wealth of tools to support each area.

With self-evaluation tools to help readers identify and celebrate current successes and pinpoint next steps for improvement, this book is an essential resource for primary school teachers, SENCOs and senior leaders who wish to ensure that their inclusive vision is embodied throughout their school.

Beccie Hawes is currently the CEO of Cadmus Inclusive – a SEN advisory support service. She is the author of four other SEN-themed books and writes extensively in this area. She has also developed educational resources to support learners with additional needs. Beccie is passionate about celebrating learning differences. Beccie strives to support schools to think differently to ensure that every pupil has the chance to shine. Beccie is a mum/stepmum to four fantastic boys and her family's dogs, Harry and Lola.

UNLOCKING INCLUSION FOR SEN LEARNERS

A PRACTICAL TOOLKIT FOR PRIMARY SCHOOLS

Beccie Hawes

Routledge
Taylor & Francis Group

LONDON AND NEW YORK

Designed cover image: © Getty Images

First published 2025
by Routledge
4 Park Square, Milton Park, Abingdon, Oxon OX14 4RN

and by Routledge
605 Third Avenue, New York, NY 10158

Routledge is an imprint of the Taylor & Francis Group, an informa business

British Library Cataloguing-in-Publication Data
A catalogue record for this book is available from the British Library

ISBN: 978-1-032-64303-8 (hbk)
ISBN: 978-1-032-63733-4 (pbk)
ISBN: 978-1-032-64307-6 (ebk)

DOI: 10.4324/9781032643076

Typeset in DIN Pro
by Apex CoVantage, LLC

Access the Support material: https://resourcecentre.routledge.com/speechmark

For my two families:
For the Hawes family – thank you for getting it and putting up with it!
Thank you for always being there and for being you. If your vibe does attract
your tribe, I'm glad it was you lot!
For my Cadmus Inclusive family – you are a bunch of smashers!
Never stop and never change!

Also for all of the tiny humans I get to work with – I hope us big
humans do a good enough job for you.

CONTENTS

Introduction   **1**

Section One **The Whole School Ethos: Developing a Dynamic, Evolving, Responsive and Inclusive Offer**   **5**

    1. Finding Out About and Responding to Our School Community's Needs   7

    2. Policy Documents   11

    3. Co-Production   13

    4. The Environment   17

    5. The Website   20

    6. How Information Is Presented   22

    7. Resources   24

    8. Access to Wider School Life   27

    9. Rules and Expectations   30

    10. The Profile of SEN   33

    Bringing It All Together   35

Section One The Toolkit   37

Section Two **The Environment: Creating the Inclusive Classroom – Environmental Design**   **71**

    1. Meeting Sensory Needs   72

    2. Display   76

    3. Access to Resources that Support Learning   80

    4. Supporting Pupils Who Are Visually and/or Hearing Impaired   83

    5. The Furniture   88

    6. Supporting Rules and Routines   91

    7. Environmental Visual Supports   95

    8. The Feeling   98

Section Two The Toolkit   101

Contents

**Section Three Teaching and Learning: High-Quality
Adaptive Teaching**   **133**
    1. Lesson Planning   135
    2. Supporting Pupils with Cognition and
       Learning Needs   137
    3. Supporting Pupils with Communication and
       Interaction Needs   140
    4. Supporting Pupils with Social, Emotional and
       Mental Health Needs   144
    5. Supporting Pupils with Physical and/or Sensory Needs   148

Section Three The Toolkit   152

So What Now? Maintenance and Innovation Planning   **171**

Glossary   173
Bibliography   176

INTRODUCTION

Being included in a meaningful and intentional sense is often the key that can unlock access to education, which then opens the doors to achieving a better and brighter tomorrow. This is particularly important for learners who have special educational needs (SEN). For these learners, how they access high-quality teaching and the wider school experience can sometimes be an unintentional afterthought.

At a time when budgets are tight, pressures on staff are mounting, time is limited and the complexity and number of pupils with special educational needs in our classrooms is ever increasing, it is more challenging than ever to offer the types of support that we believe our pupils need and deserve. The expectation is that the majority of our pupils' needs will be met in the mainstream classroom through high-quality adaptive teaching. This is filtered through to classrooms as part of a whole school approach. However, anecdotal evidence suggests that although many teachers are willing to learn professional guidance, experience and confidence are lacking. This is all then compounded by the continued 'hangover' from periods of national lockdown as a result of the Covid-19 global pandemic.

With the mantra of 'crucial for some but useful for all', what follows is designed to support you in unlocking inclusion for all but with an emphasis on pupils with special educational needs. This approach is a bit like having a shared family calendar with automatic event reminders. This is useful for the whole family so that everyone has the same information about who is doing what, when and where – everyone can then plan accordingly as they know what's going on. The calendar and its reminders could be especially helpful for busy care givers who are trying to juggle work appointments, making sure children are in the right place at the right time at the same time, as well as coordinating the shopping, health appointments and a personal life. But, in addition to this, the family calendar could be crucial for the person in the family who is autistic. They have the vital information about who, what, where and when that limits their anxiety, which then impacts positively on their overall well-being. It is all about creating a level playing field within a culture that fosters success for everyone.

DOI: 10.4324/9781032643076-1

1

How does it work?

The following three sections are designed to help you focus upon:

1. The whole school ethos – developing a dynamic, evolving, responsive and inclusive offer;
2. Creating the inclusive classroom – environmental design;
3. Teaching and learning – high-quality adaptive teaching.

In each section there is some background information and a self-evaluation tool split into several elements. Using the self-evaluation tools for each section, you will be able to identify your current position, celebrate the strengths of your school and then explore where to go next in order to develop your inclusive offer.

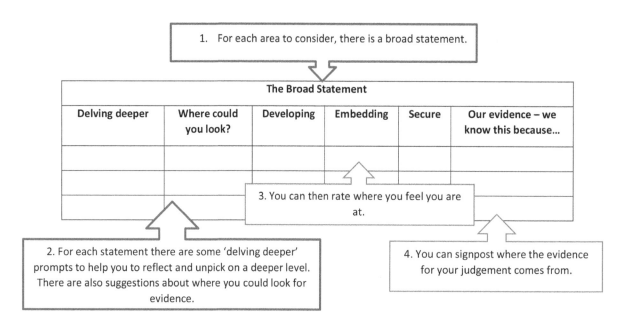

When you rate where you feel you are right now, you can identify whether your policy, procedures and practices are:

* Developing – something that you may be considering developing and putting in place.
* Embedding – something that is in place that you are working to embed in your day-to-day school life.
* Secure – something that is embedded and lived in all aspects of day-to-day school life.

After each self-evaluation tool there are some simple, cost-effective, easy-to-action but highly impactful ideas offering things that can be implemented on your journey to make intentional inclusion a reality. There isn't a tool for each individual item, but what is provided can offer a useful starting point and be adapted and developed to cover many different areas.

Finally, you can draw together the areas you wish to develop and embed into a maintenance and innovation plan (an action plan of sorts). This will enable you to strategically develop a dynamic, evolving and whole school inclusive ethos and environment that is responsive to the needs of your children and/or young people and inclusive classrooms through environmental design and high-quality adaptive teaching. This will be crucial for meeting the needs of pupils with SEN but of benefit for all.

When working through all of this it is important to remember that you can't do everything all at once. To make this manageable, you may like to:

❖ Choose only one area of one of the evaluation tools at a time and focus solely upon that,
❖ Complete all of the evaluation tools and then prioritise what you consider to be the key areas for development in order to form an action plan or, as you will see later, a maintenance and innovation plan,
❖ Set up a working party and divide up the self-evaluation tool. This could work particularly well as you could triangulate many different perspectives.

Section One

THE WHOLE SCHOOL ETHOS

Developing a Dynamic, Evolving, Responsive and Inclusive Offer

So what do we actually mean by the term ethos? The *Oxford English Dictionary* (2023) defines it as: 'the characteristic spirit of a culture, era, or community as manifested in its attitudes and aspirations'. In applying this to a school – specifically when we consider our pupils with special educational needs – it comes down to having a clear vision underpinned by strong values about what you want pupils with SEN to experience, enjoy and achieve whilst in your care. Your SEN vision and values need to be more than pithy, snappy sales pitch strap lines. They should be consistently and unapologetically lived, breathed and oozed from all aspects of school life and shared by all stakeholders. SEN must be a high-profile and integral part of your school.

To get there, consideration needs to be given to the many parts of the puzzle that contribute to your vision and values. The following self-evaluation tool will help you to explore where you are at with:

❖ Finding out about and responding to your school community's needs.
❖ Policy documents.
❖ Co-production.
❖ The environment.

DOI: 10.4324/9781032643076-2

❖ Your website.
❖ How information is presented.
❖ Resources.
❖ Wider school life.
❖ Rules and expectations.
❖ The profile of SEN.

1. Finding Out About and Responding to Our School Community's Needs

Under the Equality Act 2010 traders and service providers must remove barriers faced to access goods or services because of disability so that they can be accessed in the same way, as far as this possible, as for someone who is not disabled. This duty is called making a reasonable adjustment. These adjustments must be made if a person is disadvantaged by something because of their disability, and it is reasonable to make the changes to remove the disadvantage. This duty is anticipatory, meaning that the trader or service provider must not wait to be asked to do so. They should consider in advance what they need to do to make their services accessible to all their disabled users. So what do we mean by reasonable? The Equality and Human Rights Commission shows that it is not possible to say what will or will not be reasonable in any particular situation, but it does provide guidance on factors that may be considered when deciding what is reasonable. These include

- ❖ The needs of the user – what special educational provision might be being made for a pupil who is disabled,
- ❖ The size and resources of the provider – this includes the cost of the particular adjustment,
- ❖ The type of service required,
- ❖ How practicable and effective the changes would be,
- ❖ Health and safety requirements,
- ❖ If the change required would overcome the disadvantage experienced by the service user,
- ❖ The need to maintain academic, musical, sporting and other standards,
- ❖ If the change is what is required or is more than necessary,
- ❖ The interests of existing and future pupils.

Reasonable adjustments might include:

- ❖ Changing the way in which things are done such as rules, criteria, policies and procedures,
- ❖ Changing the physical features of the school building,
- ❖ Providing additional aids and services.

So what does this mean for your school?

The equality act applies to all schools, including special schools, publicly-funded or independent schools, pupil referral units and alternative provision academies. The schools' duties apply to early years provision and sixth form provision, where the provision is made in a school. It is the responsible body for the school that has accountability for the duties.

Whilst the institutional responsibilities lie with the responsible body, teachers have individual professional responsibilities under the Teachers' Standards (Department for Education, 2021). They 'must have an understanding of, and always act within, the statutory frameworks which set out their professional duties and responsibilities''

Disabled children and young people are covered by the SEN framework (set out in the Children and Families Act 2014) where their disability stops or makes it more difficult for them to make use of facilities that are generally provided, and they require special educational provision – something additional to or different from provision made generally for others of the same age. The definition of disability used in the SEN framework is that used in the Equality Act.

To avoid discrimination and in order to anticipate and make reasonable adjustments, schools need to know who their disabled pupils are. Understanding the challenges faced and the needs of your school's community is an essential first step to making sure that what you offer is supportive, useful and in tune with all who access your school, as well as being mindful of what might be needed in future. Although this is primarily about your pupils being able to access all aspects of school to be able to learn, it is also about your pupils' families, your staff and the wider community. The goal is to make your school feel welcoming and accessible to all. This sets the scene for an intentionally inclusive start right from the off. Thinking about what is needed right now and then proactively in the future helps to ensure that school remains an evolving inclusive environment.

There are a range of ways in which a school may become aware that a pupil may be disabled. For example: they might receive information from a pupil's previous school, they may be told by the pupil's parents or care givers, or it may be through in-school observation and assessment. Asking questions is perhaps the most obvious way of gaining this information but, with no duty in place on parents or pupils themselves to disclose a disability, it is important that questions are asked in a way that respects a pupil's dignity and privacy and encourages parents, or children and young people themselves, to share information.

It is understandable that some parents and pupils may be reluctant to share this information. They may for example worry that information might be used against their child rather than to support them to be included. It is also important to be aware that some parents may not consider their child to be disabled. It might therefore be helpful to focus upon what is needed rather than the nature or existence of a disability. The best time to have this discussion is when preparing for the admission of a pupil but it is also important to recognise that needs can change, so regular 'check ins' with all are essential.

Examples of Reasonable Adjustments in Practice

1. The class timetable is adjusted to accommodate an additional intervention for a group of pupils with learning difficulties so that they don't miss out on whole class English lessons led by their teacher. This allows time for additional rehearsal of new skills and pre-teaching of concepts to come in class.

2. A pupil with a hearing impairment sits nearer to the front of the classroom, always facing the teacher and display screen so that they are able to hear and lip- read more effectively.

3. A pupil with sensory needs is provided with a range of sensory tools to use in lessons to help them achieve and maintain an appropriately regulated state to be available for learning.

4. Where the school policy would normally provide for a three-day suspension, the policy is adjusted to provide an alternative sanction for a pupil where their behaviour is as a result their disability. The sanction reflects the gravity of the incident, is understood by the pupil, but does not involve excluding them in these scenarios.

1. Finding out about and responding to our school community's needs

Delving deeper	Where could you look?	Developing	Embedding	Secure	Our evidence – we know this because . . .
1.1 We regularly communicate with our school community to find out about the different types of special needs it has and how they feel these needs could best be supported.	• Parent, care giver and community questionnaire and/or consultation analysis. • Pupil questionnaire and/or consultation analysis. • Analysis of the school's SEN register. • Analysis of SEN specific focus groups. • Review of anecdotal evidence. • Co-production with parents, care givers and pupils.				
1.2 We make decisions about the accessibility of the school environment, how we present information and our public events based upon what we know about our school community.	• SEN Information Report and its review. • Accessibility Plan and its review.				
1.3 The transitions for pupils with SEN in to, out of and within our school are planned carefully and personalised according to their additional needs.	• SEN policy. • Admissions policy. • Transition case studies.				

2. Policy Documents

The SEND Code of Practice (Department for Education, 2015) states that governing bodies:

> must publish information on their website about the implementation of the governing body's or the proprietor's policy for pupils with SEN.

The SEN policy is a statutory document but there are no rules about what it must contain. Your policy document is in addition to the SEN information report (more on this later).

Your policy should avoid being a series of ambitions about what you want SEN to 'be like' in your school but should reflect what parents and care givers can expect their child to receive in terms of your SEN offer and what is ordinarily available on a day-to-day basis. Your policy should be available to all parents and care givers who would like a copy. Therefore, it will need to be available in a range of accessible formats.

2. Policy documents

Delving deeper	Where could you look?	Developing	Embedding	Secure	Our evidence – we know this because . . .
2.1 Within each of our policy documents there is specific reference made to how the policy is applied and adapted for pupils with special educational needs and disabilities. This supports accessibility.	• Policy documents. • SEN Information Report. • Accessibility Plan. • Governing body meeting minutes. • School quality assurance work undertaken internally and by external partners.				
2.2 When writing and reviewing our policy documents representatives from a variety of stakeholders are consulted and their views are taken into consideration.	• Pupil, parent and care giver consultation analysis. • Governing body minutes. • Reviews of anecdotal evidence.				
2.3 Policies are available in a range of formats (for example: easy-read, audio, adapted to support those with vision impairments).	• School website. • Policy documents.				
2.4 Our SEN policy has a clear SEN-specific vision and values statement that links to our overall whole school vision and values.	• Whole school vision and values. • School website. • SEN policy.				
2.5 Our SEN vision and values are evident in the day-to-day practices and procedures of school life.	• Internal and external quality assurance work (for example: learning walks).				
2.6 All school stakeholders are able to articulate the SEN vision and values from our policy and give examples of how this is 'lived' in the day-to-day life of the school.	• Internal and external quality assurance work (for example: focus groups, learning walks, subject leader monitoring).				
2.7 In line with our admissions policy, all are welcome to apply for a place at our school. If a place is available, we will undertake to use our best endeavours, in partnership with parents and care givers, to make the provision required to meet the SEN of pupils at this school.	• Admissions policy. • SEN Policy. • SEN Information Report.				

3. Co-Production

Co-production is all about doing with as opposed to doing to. The term was first used in the 1970s by the economist, Elinor Ostrom, who used the term to explain how crime rates in America dropped when the police were walking the streets, instead of patrolling them by car. When the police became more visible in the streets of local communities, they developed relationships with local people, leading to the exchange of informal knowledge that became crucial to preventing and solving crimes. It became clear that the relationship was indeed reciprocal; the police needed the communities, just as much as communities needed the police.

The process of co-production allows all involved to work collaboratively as equal partners to design, plan, deliver and review support and services in order to achieve shared outcomes. All involved are recognised as equal partners who have important contributions to make. With this in mind, careful consideration needs to be given as to how we work in partnership with our pupils and their families so that they are engaged, equal active partners in the things that impact upon them in. The co-production process can be set out as a cycle:

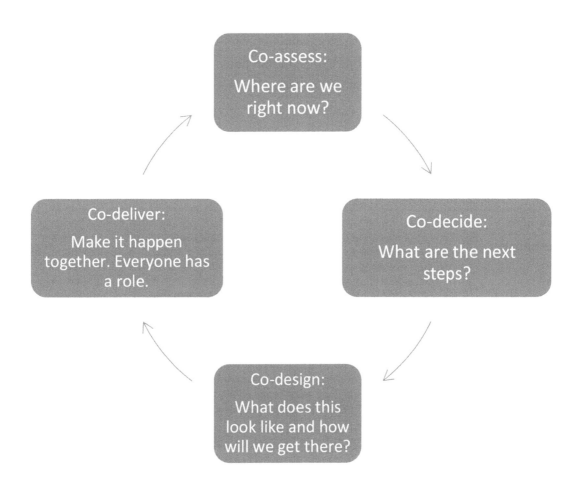

For some partners this will be an easy process to engage with but for many reasons parents, care givers and pupils can often find co-production difficult to engage with.

To achieve the destination of meaningful co-production we may need to go on a journey with our partners. In 1969, Sherry Arnstein wrote about citizen involvement in planning processes in the United States (Arnstein, 1969). In her work, she described a 'ladder of citizen participation' that showed participation ranging from high to low. Her ladder can be adapted to show the steps involved in getting there:

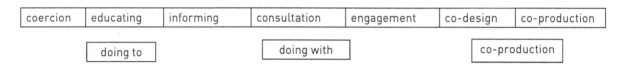

| coercion | educating | informing | consultation | engagement | co-design | co-production |

| doing to | doing with | co-production |

Co-Production in Practice

When a school was aspiring to develop their relationships with parents and care givers to shift the power dynamic from having them as a passive presence with limited engagement to becoming active, equal partners, it was recognised that asking parents and care givers to dive straight into co-production would be too much for all to manage. It was also possibly too soon in the co-production journey. Consequently, a staged plan was developed based upon the model shared in this section. It looked like this and was very successful.

Coercion	School started by inviting parents and care givers into school for fun and informal events where they could spend time learning together with their child. At these events staff would 'drop in' brief snippets of information about various things that were happening in school.
Educating	
Informing	Over time, parents were asked more frequently to share their ideas about the sorts of events they would like. Their feedback was quickly acted upon. At these events more parents were asked what they needed and felt would be helpful to them. The information shared included jargon busters, information leaflets and resource sharing, which empowered parents to access other aspects of school life with an equal knowledge base to the staff. Other opportunities to work collaboratively with staff were identified, such as volunteering to design and build a new sensory garden. A wider range of staff attended these events to breed familiarity.
Consulting	
Engagement	
Co-design	Finally, with their increased knowledge and empowerment, parents began working on further joint projects with staff. Attendance at and contributions to SEN review meetings, parents' evenings and other consultative sessions increased. Responses to activities where opinions were required also increased as parents knew their views would be listened to, valued and acted upon.
Co-production	

3. Co-production

Delving deeper	Where could you look?	Developing	Embedding	Secure	Our evidence – we know this because . . .
3.3 We consult with and involve our pupils in developing our inclusive practices. The pupils involved in this process are a representative sample of our school's population.	• Examples of pupil consultation and the resulting actions. • Policies, procedures and practices.				
3.4 We consult with and involve a representative sample of our pupils' families in developing our inclusive practices.	• Examples of family consultation and the resulting actions. • Policies, procedures and practices.				
3.5 We actively seek the views of our pupils and their families to make decisions about how our school runs on a day-to-day basis and act upon the findings.	• Pupil and family questionnaires and engagement events. • Meetings from pupil leadership meetings. • Examples of changes made to policy, procedure and practice as a result of engagement with pupils and their families.				
3.6 We proactively make adaptations to our school environment to ensure that it is accessible to all based upon what we know about our school community and its needs.	• Accessibility plan. • SEN Information Report. • Photographic evidence of changes to the school building and/or environment.				
3.7 We are pre-emptively planning ahead for what adaptations may be needed to our school building for future needs that may arise.	• Accessibility plan. • Building plans. • Budget planning documents. • Analysis of changes in our cohorts to make predictions.				
3.8 We actively make adaptations to school events to ensure that that they are accessible to all based upon what we know about our school community and its needs.	• Examples of changes made – photographic and anecdotal evidence. • Event attendance records. • Event reviews from attendees.				

(Continued)

Delving deeper	Where could you look?	Developing	Embedding	Secure	Our evidence – we know this because . . .
3.9 Parents and care givers are actively involved in assess, plan, do, review (APDR) cycles in line with the school's graduated response to SEN.	• Meeting attendance records. • APDR records. • Family conversation documentation.				
3.10 Parents and care givers feel valued and that they are active partners in their child's education.	• APDR records. • Analysis of parent/care giver questionnaires and or engagement events. • Attendance at APDR meetings and parent/care giver consultation events.				

4. The Environment

Schools and Local Authorities have to complete accessibility planning for disabled pupils. The aim of a school accessibility plan is to:

❖ Increase how much disabled pupils can participate in the full curriculum offer,
❖ Enhance the physical environment to enable disabled pupils to take better advantage of education, benefits, facilities and services provided,
❖ Develop the availability of accessible information to disabled pupils.

In achieving this, schools should have regard to the need to provide adequate resources for implementation of their plan and must review it regularly. Your accessibility plan could be a standalone document but could be included as part of another documentation such as the school development plan.

With regard to your school's environment, your accessibility plan must identify how you are improving the physical environment. This includes improvements to the physical environment of the school and physical aids to access education. The physical environment includes elements such as steps, stairways, kerbs, exterior surfaces and paving, parking areas, building entrances and exits (including emergency escape routes), internal and external doors, gates, toilets and washing facilities, lighting, heating, ventilation, lifts, floor coverings, signs, interior surfaces, room decor and furniture. Physical access-based improvements could include items such as ramps, handrails, lifts, widened doorways, electromagnetic doors, adapted toilets and washing facilities, adjustable lighting, blinds, induction loops, communication aids, well-designed (passive) room acoustics and way-finding systems. Other considerations could include the provision of low-arousal areas and improvements to the physical safety of the environment. Improved access in existing buildings can often be achieved by rearranging room space, removing obstructions from walkways, changing the layout of classrooms, providing designated storage space or reallocating rooms to particular subject specialisms. Physical aids to access education could cover computing equipment, desks and seating arrangements.

4. The environment

Delving deeper	Where could you look?	Developing	Embedding	Secure	Our evidence – we know this because . . .
	For all of the 'Delving Deeper' statements: • Accessibility policy. • SEN Information Report. • SEN Information. • Photographic evidence. • Learning walks.				
4.1 We proactively plan ahead to develop our environment for needs that may arise.					
4.2 Our environment is accessible to those who require wheelchair access.					
4.3 Signage is dyslexic friendly.					
4.4 Changes in surfaces, gradients and steps are clearly identified.					
4.5 Disabled parking is available.					
4.6 Low-arousal spaces are available for those that find it challenging to filter the environment.					
4.7 Written information is supported with visual aids to support understanding.					
4.8 Accessible toilets are available.					
4.9 Background noise is limited.					
4.10 Blackout blinds are used.					
4.11 Measures are taken to limit glare (for example: use of matt laminating wallets, background colours are strategically selected).					
4.12 Furniture is of the appropriate height for users.					
4.13 Power-assisted doors are in place to enter/exit the building.					
4.14 Alternatives to stairs are available.					

(Continued)

Delving deeper	Where could you look?	Developing	Embedding	Secure	Our evidence – we know this because . . . .
4.15 Outdoor play equipment is accessible for all.					
4.16 Images used around our school environment represent our pupils; they can 'see themselves'.					
4.17 Supportive devices to aid hearing such as hearing loops are in place.					

5. The Website

Your school website is often the very first place that people look before they physically come into school to meet you. It is also the first place that parents and care givers explore to find out valuable information about how their child's needs might be met. Consequently, it is really important that it sets the tone for how you want others to perceive your school. Many of the messages your website gives are implicit. For example, if you want others to perceive that your school is a happy and welcoming environment, is that reflected through your choice of photographs – is everyone smiling? With this in mind, it is essential to reflect upon:

5. The website

Delving deeper	Where could you look?	Developing	Embedding	Secure	Our evidence – we know this because . . .
	For all of the 'Delving Deeper' statements: • School website • Internal and external quality assurance work.				
5.1 Our school's SEN policy is available on our website.					
5.2 Our school's SEN Information Report is available on our website.					
5.3 Our school's Accessibility Plan is available on our website.					
5.4 Images used on our school website are representative of our pupils. They can: 'see themselves'.					
5.5 Information is presented in a dyslexic-friendly way.					
5.6 There is an option to have text read aloud.					
5.7 It is possible to alter the size of the information presented.					
5.8 Translation to other languages is available.					
5.9 Our website is checked at least annually to ensure that the information regarding SEN and disability: - is up to date, - has hyperlinks that work, - is easy to find, - is relevant to the needs of our community.					

6. How Information Is Presented

Schools share a wealth of spoken and written information that is often shared at a fast pace. It is essential therefore that this information is accessible to all. Consideration should be given not only to the way the information looks and/or sounds but also the content in terms of how easy it is for all to understand.

6. How information is presented

Delving deeper	Where could you look?	Developing	Embedding	Secure	Our evidence – we know this because . . .
6.1 Written information is presented using a dyslexic-friendly approach.	• Examples of written information. • School website.				
6.2 Written information is available in a range of different formats (for example: online, paper, easy-read, pupil-friendly and audio).	• Examples of the same information in a variety of different formats. • School website. • Policy documentation. • Letters.				
6.3 Written information is available in the languages spoken in our local community.	• School website. • Letters. • Examples of written information. • Policy documentation.				
6.4 Images are used to aid access to text.	• Displays. • School website. • Examples of supported written information.				
6.5 Signing is used to support the sharing of information.	• Evidence of British Sign Language (BSL) and/or Makaton use.				

7. Resources

All schools are required by law to promote the fundamental British values of:

❖ Democracy.
❖ The rule of law.
❖ Individual liberty.
❖ Mutual respect and tolerance of those with different faiths and beliefs.

Further to instilling the values of respect and tolerance for those with different faiths and beliefs we should be supporting our pupils to develop an essential understanding and acceptance of the strengths, talents, skills and needs of others. Diversity within our school communities is growing and evolving, so it is therefore essential that the resources and equipment that we have in school not only reflect the people in our schools but the wider global community too.

Our children need to see representations of who they are and who they aspire to become in today's society so that they feel a sense of belonging and connectedness. They also need to see accurate representations of their fellow humans in all of their forms so that difference is not a surprise and something that should be stigmatised. It is about celebrating people of all types in an everyday way. This extends beyond the pictures in the books that we use – it spans your whole resource collection. In 1996, the New Zealand Ministry of Education stated:

> The feeling of belonging . . . contributes to inner well-being, security and identity. Children need to know that they are accepted for who they are.

Furthermore, Osterman (2000) says a community (e.g. a school) emerges when its members experience and share a sense of belonging or personal relatedness. This leads to three crucial questions about what we offer in our schools:

❖ Can you see yourself in our school?
❖ Do you feel connected?
❖ Are you a part of it?

Step one of working out if your resources represent your pupils and are relevant to them and their lives is to know your school community well – you can revisit Section One of the self-evaluation tool for this purpose. Step two is to make sure that your community is present in and permeates through the resources that you use.

7. Resources

Delving deeper	Where could you look?	Developing	Embedding	Secure	Our evidence – we know this because . . .
7.1 Images in resources are representative of our school community and wider society.	• Displays. • Reading books. • Library books. • Textbooks.				
7.2 Textbooks are up to date.	• Textbooks. • Library books. • Reading books.				
7.3 Dolls and toys used to support play and learning opportunities allow our pupils to 'see themselves'.	• Audit of current resources.				
7.4 A range of adapted tools are available in all year groups to all pupils (for example: left-handed scissors, lightweight cutlery, triangular pencils, a range of pencil grips).	• Audit of current tools and their placement.				
7.5 Resources are labelled using words and pictures.	• Resource storage.				
7.6 Resources are housed at a level that pupils can see.	• Resource storage.				
7.7 Resources are placed in areas where pupils can see them and self-select.	• Resource storage.				

(Continued)

Delving deeper	Where could you look?	Developing	Embedding	Secure	Our evidence – we know this because . . .
7.8 Staff adapt resources to meet the needs of pupils (for example, text-based information may be copied onto an alternative colour of paper or enlarged).	• Lesson plans. • Learning walks. • Pupil voice activities. • APDR documentation.				
7.9 Specific resources are purchased matched to the needs of specific pupils.	• Lesson plans. • Learning walks. • Evidence of resources purchased to fulfil ADPR documentation, care plans and Education and Health Care Plan (EHCP) documentation.				

8. Access to Wider School Life

School isn't just about the knowledge, skills and understanding that we deliver in discrete lessons. I would argue that there are three curricula, possibly even more, that when added together, help us to meet the holistic needs of pupils:

❖ The knowledge, skills and understanding that come from discrete lessons such as learning to multiply a single-digit number by a two-digit number, writing grammatically correct sentences or comparing and contrasting the approaches of two historical leaders.

❖ There is the incidental life-based curriculum where we learn to function in the world. This might include things like making choices at lunchtime, waiting in a queue, sharing and listening to others.

❖ Finally, there is the SEN-specific curriculum. This can be additional intervention tailored specifically to a need such as a bespoke social skills programme for an autistic pupil or a specific self-esteem programme for a child with a social emotional and mental health need.

Our pupils need every opportunity to access all three curriculums in order to grow, learn and have the best possible life chances. Consequently, they need more than just access to lessons. They need to be able to access, enjoy and contribute to all aspects of the wider school life. By wider school life I refer to things like extra-curricular clubs, pupil leadership opportunities, chances to represent school, unstructured social times, school day trips, residential visits and all of the other enrichment opportunities a school can provide.

SUPPORT MATERIAL

8. Access to wider school life

Delving deeper	Where could you look?	Developing	Embedding	Secure	Our evidence – we know this because . . .
8.1 All pupils are encouraged to attend additional curricular activities such as before- and after-school clubs.	• Analysis of attendance information.				
8.2 Adaptations are made to make additional curricular activities accessible to pupils.	• Planning.				
8.3 Adaptations are made to make assemblies/gatherings accessible for pupils and the wider community.	• Evidence of adaptations such as use of Makaton signing, alternative seating arrangements, adapted written information.				
8.4 Our lunchtime and snack menu choices contain visual supports to support pupils in selecting their meal.	• Samples of menus with visual supports.				
8.5 We offer alternative places to the dining hall are available for those that need it.	• Audit of use of space at lunchtime.				
8.6 There are a variety of foods and drinks available to suit dietary requirements.	• Menus. • Audit of food/drink purchases.				
8.7 Planning for school trips accounts for accessibility requirements matched to the needs of those attending.	• Risk assessments. • Planning.				

(Continued)

SUPPORT MATERIAL

Delving deeper	Where could you look?	Developing	Embedding	Secure	Our evidence – we know this because . . .
8.8 All of our pupils are represented in pupil leadership teams.	• Pupil leadership team registers.				
8.9 All of our pupils have opportunities to represent the school in a variety of events (such as: quizzes, musical and drama performances and sporting events).	• Analysis of which children have participated.				
8.10 Visitors into our school (for example: theatre companies, guest speakers and sports ambassadors) represent diverse communities.	• Evidence of the visitors in school.				
8.11 Peer awareness and acceptance activities are in place so that pupils understand each other's needs.	• Evidence of peer awareness activity implementation. • Planning for such activities. • Timetables.				
8.12 Our school actively participates in awareness and acceptance events such as 'Autism Acceptance Week' and 'Dyslexia Awareness Week'. In addition to this, awareness and acceptance are woven throughout all aspects of school life.	• Evidence of activities in school. • Assembly plans. • Lesson plans.				

9. Rules and Expectations

The Equality Act (2010) makes it unlawful for the responsible body of a school to discriminate against, harass or victimise a pupil or potential pupil in the following ways:

❖ In relation to admissions,
❖ In the way it provides education for pupils,
❖ In the way it provides pupils access to any benefit, facility or service,
❖ Or by excluding a pupil or subjecting them to any other detriment.

There are two key concepts which act as a foundation for the duties of this act. They are:

❖ Protected characteristics,
❖ Prohibited characteristics.

The nine protected characteristics are:

❖ Age
❖ Disability
❖ Gender reassignment
❖ Marriage and civil partnership
❖ Pregnancy or maternity
❖ Race
❖ Religion or belief
❖ Sex
❖ Sexual orientation.

Prohibited conduct is a general term applied to discriminatory behaviour which is unlawful. This refers to direct and indirect discrimination, victimisation and harassment. In addition to this, the following forms of prohibited conduct apply to disabled people, including disabled pupils in schools:

❖ Discrimination arising from a disability,
❖ A failure to make reasonable adjustments.

The duties cover not just teaching and learning in classrooms, but lunchtimes and playtimes, school clubs, activities and trips – all aspects of school life!

Disabled children and young people are covered by the SEN framework where their disability prevents or hinders them from making use of facilities that are generally provided, and they require special educational provision, that is, something additional to or different from provision made generally for others of the same age. The definition of disability used in the SEN framework is that used in the Equality Act.

So, who counts as disabled?

> A person has a disability if they have a physical or mental impairment and the impairment has a substantial and long-term adverse effect on their ability to carry out normal day-to-day activities. A physical or mental impairment includes learning difficulties, mental health conditions, medical conditions and hidden impairments such as specific learning difficulties, autism, and speech, language and communication impairments.
>
> *(Equality Act, 2010)*

With all of this in mind, flexibility is crucial. It's all about considering carefully how your school rules and expectations are applied to accommodate the needs of your pupils. Simple things can be done to ensure that this takes place, such as:

❖ Allowing pupils with sensory needs alternative choices for school uniform.
❖ Adjusting your snack policy to allow a pupil with diabetes to eat at alternative times and access high-calorie snacks.
❖ Changing seating arrangements for a visually impaired pupil so that they can see teaching resources clearly.
❖ Altering timetabling for some pupils to allow them to access the dining room when it is quieter.
❖ Use of different means of recording for pupils with fine motor difficulties.
❖ Providing ear-defenders for a pupil that is sensitive to loud noises.

Often these are low-cost, high-impact changes that will make the world of difference to a pupil's ability to access all aspects of school life.

9. Rules and expectations

Delving deeper	Where could you look?	Developing	Embedding	Secure	Our evidence – we know this because . . .
9.1 Adaptations to school uniform are allowed to ensure that pupils' sensory needs can be accommodated.	• School policy.				
9.2 Adaptations to school uniform are allowed to support pupils in adhering to their cultural and/or religious beliefs.	• School policy.				
9.3 Our rewards and sanctions are applied flexibly to meet the needs of pupils with disabilities.	• Behaviour and relationships policy. • EHCP documentation. • APDR documentation.				
9.4 Our school rules are modified to account for the needs of our pupils.	• Behaviour and relationships policy. • EHCP documentation. • APDR documentation.				
9.5 Our school timetables can be altered to accommodate the needs of pupils.	• Timetables.				
9.6 Lessons are adapted across the curriculum to meet the pupils from their unique starting points.	• Lesson planning. • Policy documentation.				

10. The Profile of SEN

Special Educational Needs permeates all aspects of school life. It needs to be high on everyone's agenda. The Teachers' Standards state that:

A teacher must adapt teaching to respond to the strengths of all pupils:

❖ Know when and how to differentiate appropriately, using approaches which enable pupils to be taught effectively,

❖ Have a secure understanding of how a range of factors can inhibit pupils' ability to learn, and how best to overcome these,

❖ Demonstrate an awareness of the physical, social and intellectual development of children, and know how to adapt teaching to support pupils' education at different stages of development,

❖ Have a clear understanding of the needs of all pupils, including those with special educational needs; those of high ability; those with English as an additional language; those with disabilities; and be able to use and evaluate distinctive teaching approaches to engage and support them.

(Teacher Standard 5)

This means that the SENCO has an important role in not just being the whole school advocate for the pupils with SEN but also ensuring that SEN is a high-profile and non-negotiable aspect of school life that everyone takes a collective responsibility for.

10. The profile of SEN

Delving deeper	Where could you look?	Developing	Embedding	Secure	Our evidence – we know this because . . .
10.1 SEN is a high-profile aspect of school life.	• Learning walks. • Policy documentation. • SEN Information Report. • Governing body/ leadership team meeting minutes. • Staff meeting minutes. • Records of pupil leadership activities.				
10.2 SEN-specific continued professional development (CPD) is planned into our school improvement calendar and is accessible to all staff.	• CPD records. • CPD calendar.				
10.3 SEN 'news' is frequently shared with parents, care givers and the wider community.	• Newsletters. • School website. • School events calendar.				
10.4 SEN is part of performance management/ appraisal targets linked to the whole school development plan.	• Whole school development plan. • Performance management and/or appraisal arrangements. • School self-evaluation document.				

Bringing It All Together

Now that you have a completed self-evaluation tool it is important to decide what to focus upon. This can be a two-step process:

1. Begin by celebrating your strengths. Look back at what you have deemed to be 'secure' and the evidence that you have to support your judgements. To ensure that your judgements are secure, you consider triangulating with other viewpoints – internal and external. These are your maintenance points – things you will continue to do.

In practice

Here is an example extracted from a session in which a school was developing their maintenance and innovation plan. Senior leaders gathered together the following:

*   ❖ What they had found to be secure practice.
*   ❖ An example of outside validation – the triangulation.
*   ❖ The corresponding maintenance point.

Secure Practice	Triangulation	Maintenance Point(s)
Our continued awareness- and acceptance-raising culture (as evidenced by our participation in particular weeks but also in our on-going assembly plan, fund-raising events and curriculum).	Report from our school improvement partner visit (see paragraph two – 'Children are very understanding of each other's needs . . .').	1. To continue to actively participate in acceptance and awareness weeks. 2. To follow up participation with themed assemblies to celebrate neurodiversity.

---

2. Tease out which elements you feel are embedding and which are developing. If there are lots – prioritise. To help you to do this firstly look for the things that you feel could be of high impact but easy to implement. These are your quick wins. Then look for the stuff that is also of high impact but could be hard to do. These are the things that you will have to plan carefully for – your innovation tasks.

'Secure' Statements Maintenance Tasks	'Embedding' Statements Potential Quick Win Tasks	'Developing' Statements Innovation Tasks
For example: 3.3 We consult with and involve our pupils in developing our inclusive practices. The pupils involved in this process are a representative sample of our school's population.		
Our Priority Tasks		

You will notice that the number of priority tasks is limited. It is better to focus on a small number of tasks and do them well as opposed to trying to do everything all at once!

Section One
THE TOOLKIT

What follows is a series of tips, ideas and useable tools that link to each aspect of the self-evaluation tool. It would be impossible to implement every single tip and idea from this section. Consequently, you might like to focus on your priority tasks identified from your completed self-evaluation tool first.

DOI: 10.4324/9781032643076-3

1. Finding Out About and Responding to Our School Community's Needs

To be able to help you in making changes the following tools can be used to help:

❖ As starting point audits to help you find out more about the needs of the pupils and their families,

❖ As transition planning prompts and documents.

This tool can be used as a pupil voice activity to gather more information about the needs of your pupils. The questions are meant to be a starting point and guide and can be adapted according to the age and access levels of your pupils. There are number of ways in which you might explore them. Examples include:

❖ Pupil focus groups,

❖ Individual discussions,

❖ A written questionnaire – this can be anonymous,

❖ Pupil leadership activities – such as a pupil working party,

❖ Sent home for parents and care givers to complete with their children.

Don't forget to think about accessibility. Some pupils may need a scribe, a reader, visual supports or to answer them a few at a time over a number of different sessions.

What is it like for you to be in our school?
What makes it easy for you to be able to move around the school building to get from place to place?
What can make it difficult for you to be able to move around the school building to get from place to place?
What do you like about our school building? *Try to think about the noise levels, light levels, business, comfort, different spaces and what it can be like on different times in the school day.*
What do you not like about our school building? *Again, try to think about the noise levels, light levels, business, comfort, different spaces and what it can be like on different times in the school day.*
Are there any bits of our school that you find hard to enjoy or difficult for you to be in? Why is this? *Think about all of the different indoor and outdoor spaces.*

How easy do you find it to be able to work with the information that you are given? *Try to think about information that is said to you and information that is written down.*
Is there anything we can do to make it easier for you to be able to join in with all of the things that we offer at school? *Try to think about break and lunchtimes, special events like discos, assemblies and before/ after school clubs.*
Are there any tools or equipment that you would like to have that might make being in school and completing the work easier for you to do so independently?
Do you feel that you might have any needs that school is not helping you with yet that might make it a bit trickier for you to enjoy all that school has to offer? What might they be and what would you like school to do?

This tool is designed to gather more information to support the experiences of other stakeholders in the school. This might be the staff, the families of the pupils and other wider community members that come into contact in some way with your school. Again, the questions are meant to offer a guiding starting point and can be adapted accordingly. There are number of ways in which you might explore them. Examples include:

❖ Focus groups,
❖ Individual discussions,
❖ A written questionnaire – this can be anonymous,
❖ A form that can be completed and returned via your school website,
❖ Information collection led by your responsible leadership body,
❖ Given as part of evaluation work following a school event or gathering.

What is it like for you to be in our school?
Do you consider yourself to have any additional needs that can make coming into school challenging?
What do you think we could do to make our school building more accessible to you?
What do you think we could do to make the information that we share with you easier to access?
How easy is it for you to use our reception and entrance hall facilities?
How easy is it for you to use our bathroom facilities?
Is there anything you would like us to do to make school events like parents' evening, assemblies, school fayres and gatherings easier for you to access?

Are you able to access our school website?
Are there any tools or equipment that you would like to have available for you to use whilst in school?
Do you feel that you might have any needs that school is not helping you with yet that might make it a bit trickier for you to enjoy all that school has to offer?
What might they be and what would you like school to do?

So What? Making Decisions and Moving Forwards

Once these audit tools have been completed it is then time to consider what is needed to be done in order to act upon your findings. Some of the changes that you will make will be easy wins – small things that can be done immediately. Other things may take some strategic planning and careful consideration and potentially budget deployment. As part of creating an inclusive ethos it is important that those who took the time to share their needs with you know that their views have been heard and acted upon. A simple 'you said, so we did' could cover this:

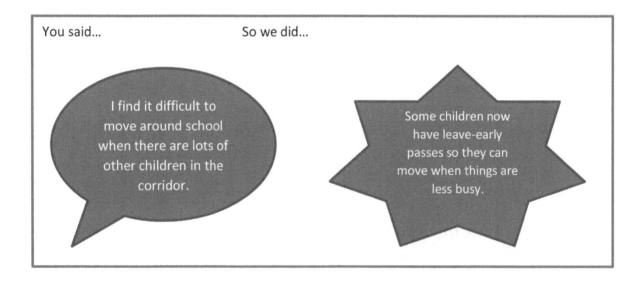

It is worth completing a needs audit annually and analysing the data that you collect to identify changes in needs and trends. This will help you to be anticipatory in planning ahead and inform the review of your accessibility plan and the actions needed to move forwards.

In being anticipatory in meeting the needs of newcomers to your school and how you might meet might those needs is essential to plan carefully for transition into your school. This checklist tool forms a useful aide memoire regarding some of the activities and information that you might like to collect to build an understanding of the reasonable adjustments and provision that you might need to offer:

Transition Aide Memoire Checklist

- ❖ Attend the pupil's annual review at their previous setting if they already have and Education and Health Care Plan (EHCP).
- ❖ Attend the review of their current assess, plan, do, review targets at their previous setting.
- ❖ Meet with the staff from the previous school setting to explore what adjustments may have been made and the success of these.
- ❖ With the parental/care giver consent ensure that you get access to relevant documentation about the pupil such as diagnostic reports, medical information, previous school records, progress updates.
- ❖ Meet with the pupil and complete the 'What is it like for you to be in our school?' tool.
- ❖ Meet with the pupil's parents/care givers to find out about the pupils needs and what they feel school will need to do to meet them.
- ❖ Allow the pupil to visit your school before joining to 'test' the building.
- ❖ Carry out a home visit to explore how the pupil accesses activities of daily living.

2. Policy Documents

The following tool will aid you in exploring your current SEN policy to ensure that it not only reflects the individuality of your school in terms of your SEN vision and values but also the staffing, procedures and approaches you deploy.

The Front Page

Include:

❖ The name and contact details of the SENCO or person responsible for managing the provision you make for children and young people with SEN.
❖ Add the status regarding the SENCO's achievement of the National Award for SEN (NASENCO award) or their NPQ SENCO qualification.
❖ State whether the SENCO is a member of Senior Leadership Team (SLT). If the SENCO is not a member of SLT, name the advocate who represents SEN on the SLT. (Ref: Role of the SENCO in Schools, SEND Code of Practice, 6.89)

Compliance

Share which statutory and guidance documents your policy has been written in conjunction with. These could include:

❖ The SEND Code of Practice 0 to 25 Years (2015)
❖ The Equality Act 2010: advice for schools DfE Feb 2013
❖ Supporting Pupils at School with Medical Conditions
❖ Working Together to Safeguard Children
❖ Keeping Children Safe in Education
❖ Teachers' Standards
❖ UN Convention on the Rights of the Child

Signpost your school policies; for example:

❖ Safeguarding Policy
❖ Accessibility Plan
❖ Subject policies

Refer to how these policies were created by the school's SENCO with the SEN Governor in liaison with the SLT, all staff and parents of pupils with SEND – refer to co-production.

Your Vision and Values

State the vision and values that drive you forwards to meet the needs of pupils with SEND. They should reflect the bigger, longer-term picture and state the aim of what you want to achieve for your pupils.

Your Objectives

This is the 'how to' section. What will you do to achieve the aim of your vision and values? This might include things like:

- ❖ To identify and provide for pupils who have special educational needs and additional needs to ensure that early identification and intervention takes place.
- ❖ To ensure that all we provide is in line with the SEND Code of Practice.
- ❖ To operate a holistic approach to the day-to-day management and provision of support for special educational needs.
- ❖ To provide a Special Educational Needs Co-ordinator (SENCO) who will provide strategic leadership for the implementation of the SEN Inclusion Policy and act as an advocate for pupils with SEN in all school decisions.
- ❖ To provide support, guidance and up-to-date training for all staff working with pupils with special educational needs.

What Is a Special Educational Need?

Make clear reference to the SEND Code of Practice's definition of special educational needs and the four broad areas of need:

- ❖ Cognition and Learning.
- ❖ Communication and Interaction.
- ❖ Physical and/or Sensory.
- ❖ Social, Emotional and Mental Health.

Remember that the purpose of identification is to work out what action the school needs to take, not to fit a pupil into a category. Your policy should make clear that at your school/setting you identify the needs of pupils by exploring the needs of the whole child and testing a hypothesis about the sorts of provision that they required.

The following should be given careful consideration but each aspect does not necessarily constitute a special educational need. However, they may have an impact upon progress and attainment.

❖ Having a disability.

❖ Having English as an additional language.

❖ The pupil's attendance and punctuality.

❖ The pupil's health and general welfare.

❖ Pupils in public care.

❖ Being in receipt of the Pupil Premium Grant.

❖ Being the child of serviceman/woman.

Your Graduated Response to SEN

This section of your policy should set out the process by which your setting/school identifies and manages children and young people with SEN. You could include:

❖ What happens before a child is placed on your SEN register? This should link with high-quality, adapted classroom teaching and some sort of early response to explore what the pupil's needs are and the provision they may require. This is the first step in responding to pupils who have or may have special educational needs.

❖ In line with the Teachers' Standards, note the responsibility that class teachers have for the progress and development of the pupils in their class, including where pupils access support from teaching assistants or specialist staff.

❖ Describe how your school/setting reviews the quality of teaching for all pupils, including those at risk of underachievement. This includes reviewing and, where necessary, improving, teachers' understanding of strategies to identify and support vulnerable pupils and their knowledge of the SEN most frequently encountered.

❖ Describe the sorts of information that you may collect to the decision to place a pupil on the SEN register.

❖ Share how your school decides whether to make special educational provision. This should involve the pupil, their family and the SENCO in considering all of the information gathered and should include high-quality and accurate assessment data, using effective tools and early assessment materials.

❖ For higher levels of need, describe your school's arrangements to utilise more specialised assessments from external agencies and professionals.

❖ Explain how the final decision is made to place pupils on the register.

❖ Describe the process followed in applying the in applying assess, plan, do review cycles.

❖ State how co-production occurs.

❖ Note how a decision will be made to cease additional/different provision if appropriate and exit the SEN register. What happens next?

Managing Pupil Need

This section should focus upon the process of how needs are managed, not the provision that is given. Here are some key considerations for you to include in this section:

❖ Make reference to the one single category of support: SEN Support.
❖ How you break down SEN Support into manageable chunks so that everyone understands the process and what happens at each part.
❖ What system for assessing, planning, delivering, reviewing and recording provision do you use?
❖ Who is the person responsible for maintaining and updating the record/plan format that you use? Lines of accountability need to be made clear.
❖ How often are plans/records reviewed and how does this contribute to pupil progress meetings?
❖ How is the type and level of provision decided?
❖ If your school/setting identifies that you are not able to fully meet the needs of a pupil through your own arrangements, what evidence do you need to identify this?
❖ Explain the process for engaging additional support/ specialist services.
❖ Who monitors the support given by outside services?
❖ When and how are pupils and their families involved?
❖ If your school/setting identify that additional funding and support are needed for a pupil from the Local Authority High Needs Block, describe what this process looks like to request an Education and Health Care Assessment.

Supporting Pupils and Their Families

In this section you could:

❖ Signpost the Local Authority local offer.
❖ Provide a link directly to the school's SEN Information Report.
❖ Identify outside agencies and services who can offer support to the family and pupil.
❖ In line with the SEND Code of Practice describe the provision that may be offered that is in addition to that which is ordinarily available (additional to and/or different from).
❖ Describe your admission arrangements and where can they be found.
❖ Describe the examination access arrangements that are relevant to your school/ setting.
❖ Explore how transition is managed – from class to class, across key stages and to another school.
❖ Provide a link to your policy on managing medical conditions.

Quality Assurance

This section should refer to your school's quality assurance procedures in evaluating the quality of provision you offer all pupils. You should set out to:

* Explain how this is achieved.
* The person with responsibility for this activity.
* Explain how evaluation and monitoring arrangements promote an active process of continual review and improvement of provision for all pupils.

Continued Professional Development and Deployment of Resources

You could include:

* How SEN is funded.
* How decisions about which resources are needed and how they are deployed are made.
* How the training needs of staff are identified and addressed.
* How the SENCO remains up to date with the changing landscape of SEN.

Roles and Responsibilities

In this section you could name and identify the role of:

* The SEN governor.
* The SENCO.
* Class teachers.
* Support staff.
* Professionals from outside services and/or agencies.
* The person responsible for managing medical needs.
* The member of staff who is the designated lead for safeguarding.

The Storage and Management of Information

This could include:

* How and where documents are stored and for how long.
* How parents and care givers can access information stored about their child.

Arrangements for Reviewing the Policy

You could detail:

❖ How you go about reviewing the policy.
❖ How often.
❖ Who is involved.

The Procedure for Dealing with Complaints

This section should link with your school/setting's comments, compliments and complaints policy and procedures. It should also detail any specific arrangements linked to special educational needs. Arrangements for how complaints are resolved and, if appropriate escalated, should be included.

Safeguarding

Detail here:

❖ The link to your school/setting's Bullying Policy and the steps that are taken to ensure and mitigate the risk of bullying of vulnerable learners at your school.
❖ Innovative ways you have in place for educating the whole school about diversity.
❖ Links to the whole school Safeguarding Policy.
❖ How to ensure that pupils with SEN have a voice which is not only heard but acted upon.
❖ Parents will want to know how you safeguard the needs of pupils with special educational needs.
❖ How you promote independence and build resilience in learning.
❖ How you adapt teaching and learning regarding sex and relationships education.

In addition to this, you may want to include specific approaches taken by the school to address specific needs of pupils.

What Should Be in the Special Educational Needs Information Report?

Information Required	✓
The aims of your provision with regard to pupils with special educational needs and/or disabilities.	
The definition of SEN and disability.	
The types of SEN for which provision is made by your school.	
The process your school uses to identify SEN.	
What a parent/care giver should do if they suspect that their child may have a special educational need.	
How your school supports pupils with SEN.	
How pupils are involved in decisions regarding provision that can better meet their needs.	
How the curriculum is adapted to meet the needs of the pupils.	
How parents and/or care givers are informed about their child's progress and achievement.	
The ways in which parents can be supported to help their child in school.	
How the school quality assures and evaluates the quality of provision for SEN.	
The support available overall to promote pupil well-being.	
How medical needs are met.	
The training that is undertaken for staff to ensure that they can meet the needs of pupils.	
How pupils are included in wider school life. For example: school trips and extra-curricular clubs.	
Arrangements for transition.	
How resources are allocated and matched to pupil need.	
How parents and care givers will be involved in planning for and meeting the needs of their child in school.	
Who should be contacted if concerns arise.	
Signposting of support services.	
Signposting of the Local Authority's Local Offer.	

When your policy and SEN Information Report is reviewed and written, consider how you make it accessible to all. Ideas for this include:

❖ Paper and electronic copies.
❖ Website access.
❖ Provision in a range of languages relevant to your school's community.
❖ Large print, Braille and audio versions.
❖ Ensuring that the font, background colour and line spacing adhere to dyslexia- friendly formats.
❖ Visual supports.
❖ An easy-read version.

3. Co-Production

Top Tips Towards Co-Production:

These tips are aimed at making sure that staff and pupils and their families have a level playing field from the start:

- ❖ Share knowledge and information in advance of meetings so that everyone has the same starting point. This avoids surprises and the feeling of being on the back foot. Things like jargon busters, having reports and agendas in advance and a clear sense of the purpose of an event will help.
- ❖ Make sure others know that you value their expertise and lived experiences.
- ❖ Use a round table so that there are no perceived sides to take.
- ❖ Make sure that information is in an accessible format for all those involved.
- ❖ Encourage everyone to contribute to the agenda for an activity, this supports a feeling of ownership.
- ❖ Use open-ended questions so that others have the chance to fully share their views.
- ❖ Make sure that those involved in co-production are truly representative of your school community.
- ❖ Listen actively and explain what actions will take place because of what you have heard.
- ❖ Make sure everyone has something to do as a result of what has been shared, with accountability built in.

A Jargon Buster

The world of Special Educational Needs has a language and series of acronyms all of its own. This reference tool can empower others to contribute as it busts that particular communication barrier. It doesn't cover everything but could be adapted.

The Special Educational Needs Jargon Buster

Term	Meaning/Definition
ADHD	Attention Deficit and Hyperactivity Disorder
APDR	Assess, plan, do, review – a cyclical approach through which a child's needs are assessed and a plan is made to address the needs identified. This can include targets, provision, intended impact and outcomes. This document will be reviewed regularly.
AS	Autism Spectrum
AT	Advisory Teacher

(Continued)

Term	Meaning/Definition
CAMHS	Child and Adolescent Mental Health Service
DCD	Developmental Coordination Delay (also known as Dyspraxia)
DLD	Developmental Language Delay
EHCP	Education and Health Care Plan
EP	Educational Psychologist
EWO	Education Welfare Officer
EYFS	Early Years Foundation Stage (Nursery and Reception class provision)
HI	Hearing Impairment
IBP	Individual Behaviour Plan
LA	Local Authority
MLD	Moderate Learning Difficulty
OT	Occupational Therapist
PD	Physical Disability
PMLD	Profound and Multiple Learning Difficulties
PRU	Pupil Referral Unit
PT	Physiotherapist
QTHI	Qualified Teacher of the Hearing Impaired
QTVI	Qualified Teacher of the Visually Impaired
QFT	Quality First Teaching
SaLT	Speech and Language Therapy
SEMH	Social, Emotional and Mental Health
SEND	Special Educational Needs and/or Disabilities
SEND CoP	Special Educational Needs Code of Practice was devised to explain the responsibilities of Local Authorities, educational establishments such as early education settings, schools and academies together with health organisations to those with special educational needs in accordance with the Children and Families Act 2014.
SENCO	Special Educational Needs Coordinator
SLD	Severe Learning Difficulties
SpLD	Specific learning difficulty – a difference or difficulty with some particular aspects of learning. The most common SpLDs are Dyslexia, Dyspraxia, Attention Deficit Disorder/ Attention Deficit (Hyperactivity) Disorder, Dyscalculia and Dysgraphia.
TA	Teaching Assistant
VI	Visual Impairment

The One Page Profile

A One Page Profile pulls together all of the essential information about a person on one piece of paper. Three deceptively simple titles are used to separate the information:

❖ What people appreciate about me,
❖ What's important to me,
❖ How best to support me.

A One Page Profile can help us to develop more effective relationships by truly understanding what really matters in someone's life and the support they will receive to live it as well as gathering a record that tells a person's story. They lend themselves well to developing a supportive initial experience in unlocking the doors to continued and effective coproduction because the views of everyone can be collected, collated and represented to make a meaningful, informative and instructive document that is highly personalised. Here is an example:

All about me.

My One Page Profile

INSERT PHOTOGRAPH HERE	**What people appreciate about me** KIND, **funny**, gentle, clever at problem solving, good at running fast, ...

What's important to me

My friends, not rushing, people explaining things slowly and giving me time to think and then ask questions, **my dog – Margo,** my special ear defenders, *going to the park on Saturday morning,* my toy teddy.

How best to support me

Don't rush me, give me my ear defenders in noisy places, give me extra time to think before you want me to answer, do not shout at me, *show me pictures when you explain something new.*

---

4. The Environment

To decide what needs to be focused upon an environmental accessibility audit could be conducted.

Environmental Accessibility Audit

School	
Completed by	
Date	

Needs to Consider		
Type of Need	Number of Pupils	Wider Community Relevance

The School Entrances/Exits			
To consider	Yes?	No?	Further comments
Are the ramps from kerbs all at level distances between the road surface and footpath with edges marked? Please consider: 1. Pedestrian crossings in and around school. 2. Parking spaces in and around school. 3. Building entrances/exits.			
There are no obstructions that block the entrances/exits to school (gates and/or doors)?			
Does the approach into school have a level surface and is it well-maintained?			
Do all external and internal doors have a clear colour contrast between the door frame and wall and door?			
Are handles and doorbells/buzzers at an appropriate height for all to access?			
Is there an option for a quiet route into and out of school for pupils that might struggle in busy and noisy environments?			
Is there tactile paving built into sloped paths and other crossing points?			

(Continued)

	Yes?	No?	Further comments
Are entrances and exits adequately lit?			
Is the reception desk/hatch at an appropriate level for all to access?			
Parking			
To consider	*Yes?*	*No?*	*Further comments*
Is there car parking for disabled people or people with reduced mobility?			
Is there an appropriate number of accessible parking spaces?			
Are accessible parking spaces clearly marked out for identification?			
Are there directions and/or signs to easily locate the accessible parking?			
Travelling Around School			
To consider	*Yes?*	*No?*	*Further comments*
Are steps highlighted with yellow or white non-slip paint?			
Are routes around school adequately lit?			
Can a pupil who uses a wheelchair move freely around the corridors and access all classrooms without encountering steps, stairs or clutter?			
Is there flexibility over lesson change times to enable pupils to move around school at quieter times?			
Are door handles fitted at a height accessible to all?			
On the opening side of the door, is there sufficient space (300mm) to allow the door handle to be grasped and the door swung past a wheelchair footplate/walker?			
Are door handles of a type that can easily be used by all people?			
Are door handrails at a height for standing/sitting use, and are door handles clearly distinguished?			
Is contrast and clarity taken into consideration in decoration. For example: floor and walls/ skirting board; door frame and wall?			
Is gloss paint avoided?			
Is the best possible achievable acoustic environment limiting background noise and reverberation provided?			

(Continued)

Signage			
To consider	*Yes?*	*No?*	*Further comments*
Do signs indicate the floor level on each floor?			
Do signs indicate the location of all places in school?			
Are signs accessible? 1. Braille. 2. Dyslexia-friendly. 3. Visually supported with pictures.			
Are signs at eye level for all to access?			
Toilet and Changing Facilities			
To consider	*Yes?*	*No?*	*Further comments*
Are toilets accessible and of a size to accommodate an appropriately sized changing couch and hoist?			
Is there a separate toilet facility provided?			
Is flooring slip-resistant?			
Are fixtures and fittings easy to distinguish by colour contrast from walls?			
Are washing and drying facilities at a height and have the access for a wheelchair user to use?			
Are all door fittings/locks easily gripped and operated?			
Are mirrors positioned at a height and location suitable for all users?			
Is the location of the different toilets clearly signed?			
Do you have a wider cubicle within the general toilets that could be used by someone with limited mobility?			
Are handrails fitted to the larger cubicle?			
Are toilet paper holders, soap dispensers of a type and location that is easily used by people with limited dexterity or movement?			
Can the emergency call system be operated from floor level?			
Are suitable grab-rails fitted in all the appropriate positions to facilitate use of the toilet?			
Are handwashing and drying facilities within reach of someone seated on the toilet?			

(Continued)

	Yes?	No?	Further comments
Are the taps appropriate for use by someone with limited dexterity, grip or strength?			
Do you have a Changing Place facility, and is it available purely for pupils/staff and external groups using the building or offered as a community facility?			
Do you offer discreet changing facilities for people that need them?			
Within the main changing area or accessible toilet, are there accessible showering facilities?			
Is there a wide shower seat or possibly two shower seats?			
Are clothes hooks/lockers of a suitable size and height to meet all users' needs?			
Are locker locks easy to use for people with limited dexterity or strength?			
Do you offer gender-neutral toilet facilities?			
Fire Procedures			
To consider	*Yes?*	*No?*	*Further comments*
Is there a visible as well as audible fire alarm system in all parts of the building, including toilets and stairwells?			
If there are no visual alarms in place, do you provide a pager system for deaf staff/pupils?			
Are fire exit routes accessible to all, including wheelchair users?			
Is evacuation from upper and lower levels possible using: 1. An evacuation lift/platform with a protected power supply? 2. Caterpillar platform lifts? 3. An evacuation chair?			
Do you provide regular evacuation training for staff which includes the person/s that will need supporting in this way?			
Do disabled staff and pupils have individual Personal Emergency Evacuation Plans (PEEPS)?			
Do you have General Emergency Evacuation Plans (GEEPS) in place for external groups, visitors and events (PEEPS)?			
Are PEEPs and GEEPs checked regularly for effectiveness and any changes in situation for the person?			

(Continued)

	Yes?	No?	Further comments
If disabled people cannot evacuate from the building independently, are designated and signed refuge areas available?			
If refuges are available, are they equipped with intercoms to let people know they are there?			
Are evacuation routes checked routinely and regularly for freedom from combustible materials/obstacles/locked doors?			
Are external fire points and routes accessible and monitored?			
Drinking Water Units			
To consider	*Yes?*	*No?*	*Further comments*
Is the area for drinking water maintained well with a level surface for access?			
Are units at an appropriate height for all to access?			
Do the taps have lever type handles?			
Functional Spaces (for example: classrooms, the dining room)			
To consider	*Yes?*	*No?*	*Further comments*
Can desks and tables be adjusted to an appropriate height for the user?			
Are visual aids and teaching resources at an appropriate height for all to access?			
Are spaces organised so that all pupils can easily access resources including, if appropriate, their own specialist resources?			
Is there adequate storage space for specialist resources and equipment?			
Is there enough space for all pupils to be able to navigate the space?			
Are the chairs provided of an adequate height and comfort level?			
Is light controllable with adequate blackout/anti-glare options?			
Is there a hearing loop?			
Are there sufficient soft furnishings to limit background noise?			
Are low-arousal spaces provided?			
Is colour and contrast taken into consideration for decoration?			
Is gloss paint avoided?			
Is furniture moveable to accommodate movement and specialist equipment?			

(Continued)

Are visual supports provided to aid access to spaces, resources and equipment?			
Are play equipment pieces (indoor and outdoor) accessible to all for independent use?			

Once this is completed, priorities can be identified and a plan formed which can contribute to your overall accessibility plan. For example:

Improving the Physical Access of the Building

Item to Address	Action	Timescale
Increasing access to accessible car parking spaces.	The two nearest car parking spaces to the door will become designated accessible bays. The caretaker will repaint these to signpost.	Completion by the end of the spring term this academic year.
Accessible toilet and changing facilities.	Adapted wash basins to be at wheelchair height with appropriate space underneath for a wheelchair user to get close to the basin.	Completion by Easter break this academic year.

5. The Website

The Statutory Checklist

For Special Educational Needs and information that links with this your website should contain:

- ❖ An SEN Information Report that is updated at least annually.
- ❖ Details of how your school complies with the public sector equality duty - you must update this information every year.
- ❖ Your school's equality objectives – you must update this at least once every 4 years.
- ❖ Details of your school's behaviour policy. This policy must comply with section 89 of the Education and Inspections Act 2006.
- ❖ The content of your school curriculum in each academic year for every subject which includes mandatory subjects such as religious education, even if it is taught as part of another subject or subjects, or is called something else, the names of any phonics or reading schemes you're using in key stage 1 and how parents or other members of the public can find out more about the curriculum your school is following. You must also set out how over time you will increase the extent to which disabled pupils participate in the school's curriculum, as part of your school's accessibility plan
- ❖ Admission arrangements.
- ❖ A statement regarding your values and ethos.
- ❖ Information on the governing body in line with statutory guidance on the constitution of governing bodies of maintained schools.

How Accessible Is Your Website?

Some Reflection Points

- ❖ Is there an option to have the text read aloud?
- ❖ Can the font style and size be altered by the user?
- ❖ Can the background and/or contrast be changed?
- ❖ Are videos and/or visual images used to aid understanding of written text?
- ❖ Is there a description of the images used to support those with visual impairments?
- ❖ Can flashing images be switched off?
- ❖ Is information well-spaced and signposted with clear headings?

- ❖ Are headings and titles descriptive of the text/topic to come?
- ❖ Is there an option to translate the text to other languages?
- ❖ Is the website easy to navigate?
- ❖ Are easy-read versions of written documentation available?
- ❖ Is there a plan for individuals who may not have access to the internet or access to appropriate viewing devices?
- ❖ Can the website be navigated using a range of tools such as a mouse, keyboard, touchpad, eye gaze software and/or switch devices?
- ❖ Are videos/sound recordings captioned?
- ❖ Are there different options for viewing media content?
- ❖ Are items grouped logically using bullet points and/or numbered lists?
- ❖ Can users adjust the timings so that there is more time available to view information that moves on?

The following tool comprises some questions that you could either give as a questionnaire or use in a conversation to ask visitors to your website how they feel about it and make any necessary improvements.

Thank you for visiting our website. We wondered what you thought about the following:

1. How easy was it to find the information that you were looking for?
2. How easy was it for you to find our SEND Information report?
3. Could you make changes to the website to suit your preferences (such as altering the font size)?
4. What do you think about the design of our website? Please comment on the colour choices, the font sizes and how well the information is spaced out?
5. Is the information in your preferred language?
6. Is the information on our website reflective of what you know about our school?
7. Did all of the links work to your satisfaction?
8. Are all of the videos captioned? Do the captions run well?
9. Are the images accessible to you?
10. Do you think that the images used are representative of our school community?
11. Is there anything about our website that we could improve?

6. How Information Is Presented

The following is a useful reminder about how written information is presented to your pupils and their families. Often, we have really good intentions about making things look stylish and beautiful but, what we do from a good place, can hinder access to written materials.

Fonts with lots of serifs (fancy flicks) can look really stylish but the brain has to work harder to 'clean up' which slows down processing time. That is why a more rounded font is easier to read. It takes a lot less work!

Think carefully about contrast.

Pastel backgrounds with a dark coloured test works well.

Text layout is important.

- Use bullet points.
- Separate with spaces.

Complicated layouts make it harder to read.

Use logical, linked images to aid understanding.

Making Changes that Benefit Everyone – An Example in Practice

A pupil who I observed in a classroom experienced visual stress and slow visual processing challenges. I asked his teacher if the background colour on the interactive display board could be altered so that it was a buff pastel colour. I also asked her to double space the information and to use a rounded font with a dark coloured text.

After a week, I revisited the pupil who shared that: 'I can read the information on the board loads better now, Miss. It is so much clearer. I get less tired. My friends like it better the way you said too.'

When I asked his friends about this, one of them shared that: 'It is just clearer. I prefer it the new way. It is easier to read and find your way around.'

Getting the Message Across: Top Tips for Effective Communication

Allow additional thinking time for what you have said to be processed.

Repeat what you have said in exactly the same format so that the receiver doesn't need to reprocess from the very beginning.

What might it be useful to share beforehand? Think about challenging vocabulary or pre-teaching and exposure opportunities.

Use plain English – keep jargon and specialist terms to a minimum.

Where possible use visual images and/or signing to support understanding.

7. Resources

Finding out more about your resources:

It would be practically impossible to explore every single resource in detail in your school's setting. The following points may help to provide a focus:

1. **Decide on some criteria**: What data will you be looking for? The concepts of diversity and inclusivity are broad spectrums that could be difficult to define.
2. **Start with a random sample**: Try collecting the nearest ten resources from a particular genre such as 'textbooks' and using those to extrapolate. For example, if only one of your ten books features a neurodiverse character, you can reasonably deduce that this will apply to approximately 10% of your stock. This approach could then be further applied to other genres such as dolls.
3. **Look at your school displays**: Are they representative of your school community and the wider world? Consider the images, resources, publications and quotes that represent the people of the world that we live in.

Can you see yourself?
Book reflections

Characterisation
Are the characters in the book thoughtfully developed individuals with agency?
Is characterisation authentic?
Do the characters live an everyday life?
Does the book challenge or reinforce misconceptions about an under-represented group?
Does the dynamic between characters suggest a problematic hierarchy with reference to difference?

Illustration
Are the illustrations of characters of a high quality, resulting in characters that are relatable?
Do the illustrations of characters embody agency?
How do props, background and other visual cues add to developing an understanding of the character and their world?

Plot
Is the character's needs or difference incidental to the narrative?

> Is the plot driven by the character's difference? If so, is this necessary to furthering the storyline and appreciation of the character and their world?
>
> Does the plot better support the reader to identify with and understand points of difference?

When thinking about resources – particularly how pupils might access adapted tools for the job – the following isn't so much of a tool. It is more of an example that you could adapt and apply in your own setting.

Accessing Adapted Tools and Aids: An Example in Practice

When observing a child in their classroom to find out more about how we could best support them, it became clear that to be able to access learning tasks with greater independence access to the following was needed:

❖ Adapted scissors,
❖ Larger triangular pencils,
❖ A larger triangular pen,
❖ Use of a writing slope,
❖ A seating wedge.

When this was discussed, the pupil was very reluctant to be seen using these things as he did not wish to present as appearing different to his peers. With his consent we took the following approach:

❖ The scissors, pen and pencils were put in the same pencil/scissor pots as non-adapted tools on all tables. Nothing was said, but it was hoped that the pupils would infer that they were there for everyone to use.
❖ Four writing slopes and four seating wedges were placed out on a shelf in the classroom in open view of everyone. The class teacher explained to the class what they were for, how they should be used and why they may be of benefit to some pupils.
❖ Nothing more was said or done.

What happened?

- ❖ For the first few days, several children began to experiment with the using the adapted tools and additional aids. This spurred our focus pupil on and he began to use them too.
- ❖ Over time, many pupils stopped using the tools but those that really needed to and felt they were of benefit continued. This included the focus pupil.
- ❖ The focus pupil's independence increased and he found accessing certain classroom tasks independently easier.

What did we learn?

- ❖ When offering adapted tools and aids, building in an approach which allows for choice and control is integral to gaining more consistent and impactful use.

8. Access to Wider School Life

The following are some reflection statements which could help you to identify how your accessible wider school life activities are.

- ❖ Do pupils with additional attend after school/before school and lunch time extracurricular provision/clubs? If so, do they attend a wide range of clubs and are a number of different children attending or is it the same few?
- ❖ Do pupils with additional needs attend special events such as discos and school fairs?
- ❖ Are a wide range of your school community members represented in pupil leadership activities?
- ❖ Do children with additional needs have opportunities to represent the school in activities such as quizzes, sports matches and community events?
- ❖ How active are pupils with additional needs in participating in school showcase events such as open evenings?

Busting Barriers: An Example in Practice

Often it is the small things that can make a massive difference.

At a review meeting, it was noted that a pupil with special educational needs was not accessing any of the additional curricular activities on offer. When asked about this the pupil responded with: 'I want to go to computing club but I can't remember the logins and the passwords. Sometimes my eyes hurt because the writing on the screen moves about. It can all be a bit fast too, so I am not sure what to do.'

The school made some very simple but powerful accommodations:

- ❖ Providing a peer buddy to help with logging in.
- ❖ The background colour of the computer screen was changed.
- ❖ The pupil was offered rest breaks to move away from the screen.
- ❖ A visual timeline was created for each club session.

Following this, the pupil didn't miss a single session!

9. Rules and Expectations

It is difficult to provide a simple, 'catch all' tool that will help with this. It is more of a thought process that is required for each pupil and their unique situation and needs. It is important to remember that the reasonable adjustments duty is triggered only where there is a need to avoid 'substantial disadvantage'. 'Substantial' is defined as being anything more than minor or trivial. Whether a pupil is at a substantial disadvantage or not will depend on the individual situation. Here are some useful examples and possible solutions that will provide you with some useful benchmarking tools for your school and pupils.

Rules and Expectations: Benchmarking

The issue	Is the pupil at a disadvantage?	Flexibility – What can you offer?
A disabled pupil with severe manual dexterity difficulties finds it difficult to write large amounts of text by hand and so this takes him considerably longer than other pupils.	This depends on the nature of recording or pupil feedback within a lesson. In lessons where there is a lot of writing – yes. This wouldn't be the case in a lesson where pupils provided oral feedback.	• Avoid copying lots of written information – the pupil could be given a copy to highlight key points on. • Offer a scribe. • Offer rest breaks. • Use alternative means of recording such as tables and diagrams. • Alter expectations for the quantity of written output.
A visually impaired pupil who can see material only in 16pt font or larger.	Yes.	• Enlarge resources for the pupil to their required font size. • Change seating arrangements so that the pupil can see teaching resources. • Carefully review the reading books offered looking at accessibility.
A pupil with chronic fatigue syndrome finds it harder to concentrate in lessons in the afternoon as a result of an increase in her tiredness.	Yes – particularly in afternoon lessons.	• Alter expectations about participation and work output for afternoons. • Allow rest/respite breaks. • Consider the school timetable carefully – perhaps English and mathematics should be taught only in the mornings.
A pupil has severe eczema which is exacerbated by the particular fabric used in the uniform trousers.	Yes.	• Allow the pupil to wear trousers made from an alternative fabric.

10. The Profile of SEN

SEN Butterflies: Raising and Maintaining the Profile

Butterflies are remarkable creatures. They flutter in, often causing everyone to stop in their tracks to observe and admire them, and then gracefully flutter out. When they have gone, people often comment upon their beauty – they leave a lasting impact. Brief but beautiful! This approach is something that you could use in every staff meeting. It works like this:

1. Take five minutes of every staff meeting to share one short, succinct but powerful 'butterfly'. This is a simple statement which the SENCO or a colleague shares that is SEN-focused. The statements could be:

    ❖ Latest SEN statistics and data linked to your school.
    ❖ A top tip to improve practice/provision.
    ❖ An inspirational teaching and learning quote related to SEN.
    ❖ A pupil or parent comment that draws attention to how they can be best supported.
    ❖ A resource recommendation.
    ❖ A useful website.
    ❖ A helpful organisation to follow on social media.

2. Each 'butterfly' is collected and displayed in a staff shared space as a permanent reminder (above the photocopier works well for this or on the back of the toilet – people will read whilst they are doing what they need to do).

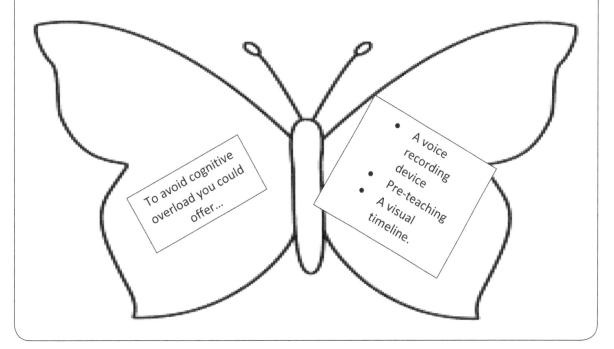

The Golden Thread

There is a connection between whole school development planning, staff appraisal and continued professional development (CPD). By making SEN of a high profile within these important aspects of school leadership and management tasks, its importance and profile within the school cannot be argued! A 'golden thread' should run through all three.

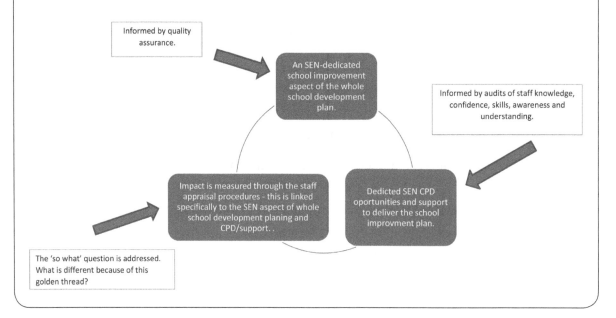

Sharing with the Wider Community

The profile of SEN needs to be high not just in school but with the wider community such as parents, care givers, governors and people that live in the local area. An SEN Celebration newsletter can do just this. It is important to have physical and digital copies which could be shared on your school website which could be half termly. This should be sent to all stakeholders, not just those with a direct SEN connection.

Aims

- ❖ To provide a 'round-up' of good news about all things SEN in school.
- ❖ To provide a non-threatening communication that shares valuable SEN information.
- ❖ To ensure that the profile of SEN and how it operates in school is high-profile.

When?

A half-termly publication.

Format

❖ Digital – website and school app.

❖ Physical – paper copies.

Potential Content

❖ Pupil spotlights – sharing of excellent work, performances, demonstrations of school values, pupil achievements and contributions.

❖ Professional spotlights – profiles that explain who they are and what they do – focusing on the SEN team in school and visiting professionals.

❖ Explanations of interventions and specialist resources used in school.

❖ Signposting of resources and services.

❖ Signposting of useful websites and social media pages.

❖ Top tips to support pupils at home.

❖ Information about review meetings and SEN special events in school.

❖ Awareness-raising articles.

❖ Pupil-led articles.

❖ Parent-written articles.

Where Does This All Lead To?

Once you have a firm idea of what you want your inclusive offer to look like, it needs to come together in a vision statement that yells what you are selling. Remember, it is all well and good to have a strong vision statement; it has to be lived and brought to life through day-to-day practice. I think the following does the job nicely:

The SEN Vision: An Example in Practice

Here is a real example of an SEN vision developed by a primary school:

> We offer our SEND children a rich, broad and balanced curriculum delivered with high expectations and aspirations for all. Learning is not limited for any child. We seek to ensure that our children have a strong sense of belonging and connection to our St Giles family so that they leave with the cultural capital required to be 21st century citizens. Every child is celebrated.
>
> (St Giles CofE Primary School, Walsall)

Section Two
THE ENVIRONMENT

Creating the Inclusive Classroom – Environmental Design

I have the pleasure and privilege of going into so many different classrooms. Each one is a unique place. I marvel at the hive of activity, the buzz of learning and the exciting magic, sparkle moments when a pupil's life changes forever because they have learnt something new. It is difficult to identify what a 'magical' classroom looks like; there is no checklist. I think it is a feeling – a 'gut reaction'.

Here's the contradictory part. Despite me saying that this is not about a checklist, there are lots of practical things that we can put in place that will help us to create the optimal, inclusive conditions for learning.

As with Section One, what follows is a self-evaluation tool that will help you to explore the following elements:

- ❖ Meeting sensory needs.
- ❖ Classroom display.
- ❖ Access to resources that support learning.
- ❖ Supporting pupils who are hearing and/or visually impaired.
- ❖ The furniture.
- ❖ Supporting rules and routines.
- ❖ Environmental visual supports.
- ❖ The feeling.

DOI: 10.4324/9781032643076-4

1. Meeting Sensory Needs

Do you ever have one of those days where you feel a bit 'out of sync'? I often describe this sensation as being out of balance. This can be because our sensory needs are not being met. We have times when we just need something – this can be referred to as being sensory seeking. There are other times when things feel a bit too much to manage – this can be referred to as being sensory avoiding. We can flit between these two states throughout the day. For some learners, it can be challenging to strike a balance so that they have the appropriate arousal state to be available for learning.

We all have several senses – not just the famous five that we are all aware of. For the purpose of learning and supporting children to meet their own sensory needs, I will be focusing upon the following:

Sense	Some Things to Consider
Sight (visual)	• Is a dominant sense. • Allows us to connect with our surroundings and helps us to remain safe. • Collects environmental data which is sent to the brain for processing.
Hearing (auditory)	• Can be unconscious and conscious. • Helps us to 'tune in' and focus. • Can help us to identify threats before we see them. • Our hearing levels can fluctuate.
Smell (olfactory)	• Closely linked to taste. • Can help us to detect if something isn't 'quite right'. For example, foods that have gone off and may make us ill.
Taste (gustatory)	• Via our tongue. • Closely linked to smell. • Helps us to detect danger (for example – recognising potentially harmful substances).
Touch (tactile)	• Through our skin, provides the largest external sense. • Is generally outside of our body but also helps us identify temperature. • Supports precision of motor skills (for example: using tools for learning such as a ruler, pencil and scissors. • Triggers movement away from danger (for example – recoiling quick if you touch something plate). • Helps us to process and understand size, shape, texture of objects and people in the environment. • Allows us to recognise pain.
Proprioception	• Is your awareness of the position and movement of your body within a space. • Mostly an unconscious sense. • Supports us with judging movement and force. • Without it we rely on visual input. • Helps us to access all motor- based tasks. • Supports our spatial awareness.
Vestibular	• Is located within our inner ear. • Provides our brain with information about: motion, the position of our head, spatial orientation, balance and maintaining posture.
Interoception	• Essential for supporting us with recognising and understanding what is happening inside our own body. • Required for self-regulation so that we can reach an appropriate arousal level for learning. • Pupils need interoceptive awareness so they can recognise and plan for things such as visiting the toilet or understanding the difference between feeling physically sick and feeling anxious.

If our learning environments are sensory-friendly then our pupils will find it much easier to feel balanced and in the right state for learning.

1. Meeting sensory needs

Delving deeper	Where could you look?	Developing	Embedding	Secure	Our evidence – we know this because . . . .
1.1 A range of sensory tools (such as fidget tools) are available for our learners to access as and when needed to support self-regulation.	• Can they be seen in learning environments? • Learning walk records. • Environmental audits.				
1.2 Sound and lighting levels can be altered to suit the needs of learners (for example blinds can be drawn).	• Environmental audits. • Learning walk records.				
1.3 Our seating plans are flexible so that pupils can move away from sensory experiences that they may find difficult to filter.	• Environmental audits. • Learning walk records.				
1.4 Reflective surfaces are kept to a minimum to avoid glare.	• Environmental audits. • Learning walk records.				
1.5 Our learning environments are well ordered and organised.	• Environmental audits. • Learning walk records.				
1.6 Sudden, loud noises are minimised where possible (such as bells and alarms).	• Environmental audits. • Learning walk records. • Timetables.				

(Continued)

Delving deeper	Where could you look?	Developing	Embedding	Secure	Our evidence – we know this because . . .
1.7 We give careful consideration to things that may create odours (for example cleaning products).	• Environmental audits. • Caretaking records. • Timetabled cooking activities.				
1.8 Varied seating options are available.	• Environmental audits.				
1.9 Movement times between locations in school are flexible to avoid crowds and noise.	• Timetables. • Learning walk records.				
1.10 Our queuing and waiting systems are flexible to avoid crowds and noise.	• Timetables. • Learning walk records.				
1.11 We have low arousal spaces available for withdrawal too when needed.	• Environmental audits. • Learning walk records. • Can the space be identified?				

2. Display

Classroom display offers a wealth of opportunity for us to:

❖ Support learning through providing models to check against, supports to scaffold learning and reminders of key facts and information.
❖ Celebrate progress and achievements.
❖ Promote a sense of belonging.
❖ Inspire.
❖ Signpost.

It could be argued that the right kind of displays are:

❖ Stimulating.
❖ Inviting.
❖ Inspiring.
❖ Representative of those accessing them.
❖ Celebratory.
❖ Informative.

They must also be inclusive and accessible to all.

2. Display

Delving deeper	Where could you look?	Developing	Embedding	Secure	Our evidence – we know this because . . .
2.1 We showcase pupil work from a range of abilities and individuals on our displays.	• Learning walk records. • Environmental audits.				
2.2 Our displays contain useful and current scaffolds that will support learning (for example: mathematical processes for the current pencil and paper strategy being taught) for pupils of all abilities.	• Environmental audits. • Learning walk records.				
2.3 For current topics, key information and reminders of important facts are displayed.	• Environmental audits. • Learning walk records.				
2.4 Pupils are able to tell us about what is on the walls and why it is helpful.	• Environmental audits. • Learning walk records. • Pupil voice activities.				
2.5 Lettering is clear and a rounded font is used. All letters stand out from the display background.	• Environmental audits. • Learning walk records.				
2.6 The information on display can be clearly seen from all positions within the environment.	• Environmental audits. • Learning walk records.				
2.7 Reflective surfaces are kept to a minimum (for example: matt laminating wallets are used to avoid glare).	• Environmental audits. • Learning walks.				

(Continued)

Delving deeper	Where could you look?	Developing	Embedding	Secure	Our evidence – we know this because . . .
2.8 Information is not placed directly in front of a light source (for example: information is not stuck to windows).	• Environmental audits.				
2.9 Colour schemes are carefully considered so that there is an appropriate level of contrast between the written information and background.	• Environmental audits. • Learning walks.				
2.10 Displays are well organised and not cluttered.	• Environmental audits. • Learning walks.				
2.11 Pupils are able to find what they are looking for easily and independently.	• Environmental audits. • Learning walks. • Pupil voice activities.				
2.12 Images and/or objects of reference are used to support the meaning of key vocabulary.	• Environmental audits. • Learning walks.				
2.13 Images are representative of a broad range of members of society and reflect the school community.	• Environmental audits. • Learning walks.				
2.14 Voice-recording devices are used to provide description.	• Environmental audits. • Learning walks.				

(Continued)

Delving deeper	Where could you look?	Developing	Embedding	Secure	Our evidence – we know this because . . .
2.15 There is an option for learners to remove part of the display to take to their table and then return – this limits difficulties with copying.	• Environmental audits. • Learning walks.				
2.16 Displays promote belonging. For example: photographs of pupils are included, use of welcome signs.	• Environmental audits. • Learning walks.				
2.17 Tools that can support learners with organisation are displayed such as: visual timelines, task checklists, equipment checklists.	• Environmental audits. • Learning walks. • Monitoring of the implementation of individual 'do' requirements from assess, plan, do, review (APDR) documentation.				

3. Access to Resources that Support Learning

Part of being an effective learner is being able to know when you need a particular resource to support you in achieving an outcome or when to access tools for the job that will help with accessibility. For example, if you have lots of complicated numbers to add you might decide to use a calculator. This would help you to achieve an accurate outcome. But, if you are finding that your writing tool is uncomfortable to hold, you might decide to use a pencil grip. This would aid your writing stamina and comfort level, making the task easier to access.

What is important here is that not only do we have the resources that our pupils may require, but that they are accessible so that our learners have the opportunity to:

* Select the resource that they need by making a considered choice.
* Use the resource effectively and independently at the right time.

It is also important that consideration is given to the personalised resources that some learners might require. Often, I am told by pupils that they know they need a particular resource to aid their access to learning, but they are reluctant to use it as they feel anxious about being perceived to be different from their peers. We need to explore how these types of resources can be provided in a way in which difference isn't a thing that causes anxiety.

This all forms an essential part of our learning environment.

3. Access to resources that support learning

Delving deeper	Where could you look?	Developing	Embedding	Secure	Our evidence – we know this because . . .
3.1 Resources are located and stored in places that pupils can access freely and independently at appropriate times during the lesson.	• Environmental audits. • Learning walk records. • Pupil voice activities.				
3.2 Our resources are clearly labelled with words and supporting images/objects of reference.	• Environmental audits. • Learning walk records.				
3.3 Our pupils are actively encouraged to independently consider and choose which resources they need to support their learning independently.	• Learning walk records. • Pupil voice activities. • Lesson planning.				
3.4 A range of adapted and alternative tools are available for a range of skill levels. These are available for all to use.	• Learning walk records. • Lesson planning. • Resource inventories.				
3.5 Resources on offer allow for the development of skill progression from the pupil's unique starting point.	• Learning walk records. • Environmental audits. • Lesson planning. • Resource inventories.				

(Continued)

Delving deeper	Where could you look?	Developing	Embedding	Secure	Our evidence – we know this because . . .
3.6 Pupils can use the resources provided with independence.	• Learning walk records. • Lesson planning. • Pupil voice activities				
3.7 Our pupils respond positively to and are accepting of the additional resources that they are offered.	• Learning walk records. • Resource inventories.				
3.8 A range of resources are on offer to support a broad variety of needs.	• Learning walk records. • Environmental audits. • Resource inventories.				
3.9 Resources are in good condition.	• Environmental audits. • Learning walk records. • Resource inventories.				

4. Supporting Pupils Who Are Visually and/or Hearing Impaired

Vision impairment in children and young people is a low-incidence but high-impact disability that can take many forms. The impact upon learning can be very different to each pupil, depending upon the severity and incidence.

The impact of having a visual impairment on a pupil's development depends on many factors, including the severity, type of loss, the age at which the condition occurs and overall functioning level of the child/young person. Many pupils who have multiple disabilities also have hearing and visions impairments. It is important to remember that wearing glasses which improve vision or having difficulties with colour vision alone may not necessarily result in the formal identification of a special educational need. Significant vision impairment can delay early childhood development and learning, including social communication, mobility and everyday living skills.

It could be argued that most teaching approaches take vision for granted, so making sure that visually impaired pupils achieve their full educational potential can be challenging. Consequently, specialist advice and support from qualified teachers of children with vision impairment (QTVI) which is often accessed through the local authority may be required.

Hearing impairment can have a significant impact on the educational development of pupils and in some cases result in learning delays and reduced curricular access. Hearing impairment spans a range from mild/moderate to severe/profound. It can be temporary, fluctuate or permanent.

In the ideal world, most pupils with a hearing impairment will have been diagnosed at the pre-school stage and will have accessed some level of support from their local Hearing Impairment Team and health professionals. It is possible for some pupils to acquire hearing loss late in life through accident or illness or a genetic condition.

A significant proportion of pupils have some degree of hearing difficulty at some time. Temporary hearing loss in the early years is often caused by the condition known as 'glue ear'. Such hearing losses can fluctuate and may be mild to moderate in degree and can compound other learning difficulties.

Occasionally, a significant hearing loss may be caused by a long-term conductive loss in both ears. Significant permanent hearing losses are usually bilateral (both ears) and sensori-neural (due to problems with the auditory nerve or the cochlea) in their origin. These may be severe or profound and may give rise to severe and complex communication difficulties.

A permanent loss in one ear and a temporary loss in the other may also cause significant hearing impairment.

Listening to language through hearing aids and cochlear implants and the visual concentration required following lip reading and sign language can be very tiring. Studies have shown that deaf students are also at higher risk of developing social and emotional difficulties compared to hearing peers.

Many students with hearing impairment may require some of the following:

❖ Flexible teaching arrangements;
❖ Appropriate seating, favourable acoustic conditions and lighting;
❖ Adaptations to the physical environment of the school;
❖ Adaptations to school policies and procedures;
❖ Access to alternative or augmented forms of communication;
❖ Access to amplification systems;
❖ Access to areas of the curriculum through specialist aids and equipment;
❖ Regular access to specialist support from the Hearing Impairment Team.

It is therefore essential that we get our learning environments right for these pupils so that they have the best possible support and opportunity to flourish!

4. Supporting pupils who are hearing and/or visually impaired

Delving deeper	Where could you look?	Developing	Embedding	Secure	Our evidence – we know this because . . .
4.1 Measures are in place to reduce background noise where possible (for example: closing windows and doors to block sound as appropriate).	• Environmental audits. • Learning walk records.				
4.2 Measures are in place to reduce extraneous and/or unnecessary noise in the classroom (for example: turning off projectors when not in use).	• Environmental audits. • Learning walk records.				
4.3 Pupils are encouraged to minimise noise where possible (for example: by moving through school quietly).	• Environmental audits. • Learning walk records.				
4.4 Improvements to the quality of sound within the classroom have been made (for example, sticking soft pads on the bottom of chairs and table legs, using fabrics to reduce hard surfaces, and installing improved ceiling tiles or acoustic clouds).	• Environmental audits. • Learning walk records.				
4.5 Flexible seating arrangements are in place so that learners can move to sit nearer and/or further away from noise sources.	• Environmental audits. • Learning walk records.				

(Continued)

Delving deeper	Where could you look?	Developing	Embedding	Secure	Our evidence – we know this because . . .
4.6 Resources to support hearing are in good condition and working order.	• Environmental audits. • Learning walk records. • Resource inventories.				
4.7 Resources to support the understanding of language are in place (for example: visual cues/images and/or objects of reference).	• Environmental audits. • Learning walk records.				
4.8 Teaching staff do not stand in front of light sources when communicating.	• Environmental audits. • Learning walk records.				
4.9 Furniture is kept in a consistent place. When it is moved, pupils are given the opportunity to re-orientate themselves.	• Environmental audits. • Learning walk records.				
4.9 Cupboard doors and drawers are kept closed.	• Environmental audits. • Learning walk records.				
4.10 Tripping hazards are kept to a minimum (for example: all chairs are tucked under tables).	• Environmental audits. • Learning walk records.				
4.11 Resources are stored in a consistent location and are clearly labelled with print, pictures and/or objects of reference in an accessible format.	• Environmental audits. • Learning walk records.				

(Continued)

Delving deeper	Where could you look?	Developing	Embedding	Secure	Our evidence – we know this because. . . .
4.12 Classroom displays incorporate voice recording devices with added description that can be played to increase accessibility.	• Environmental audits. • Learning walk records.				
4.13 Measures are in place to eliminate or reduce glare such as use of matt laminating wallets.	• Environmental audits. • Learning walk records.				
4.14 Lighting levels can be adjusted.	• Environmental audits. • Learning walk records.				
4.15 Flexible seating arrangements are in place so that learners can move to be nearer to the teacher and/or resources.	• Environmental audits. • Learning walk records.				
4.16 The print size of text and images on display is altered to meet the needs of those accessing them.	• Environmental audits. • Learning walk records.				
4.17 Resources available to support visually impaired pupils are in good condition and working order.	• Environmental audits. • Learning walk records. • Resource inventories.				

5. The Furniture

Furniture is an integral part of creating an inclusive classroom environment, as it can help break down physical barriers and create a welcoming space for all pupils. When it comes to classroom furniture, I think that Goldilocks had the right idea – what we offer for our pupils needs to be just right. None of us likes an uncomfortable chair and we all have different requirements for what makes the perfect mattress for the perfect night's sleep. The bottom line on this is that if our learners are not comfortable, there will be a detrimental impact upon their learning in terms of their ability to:

❖ Feel comfortable.
❖ Engage with learning tasks.
❖ Remain focused and concentrate.
❖ Be independent in selecting and accessing resources.
❖ Develop core strength which is essential for accessing learning tasks such as sitting up straight to write.

When exploring the classroom furniture we have on offer, we need to consider:

❖ The age of our pupils.
❖ The size of our pupils.
❖ The types of activity that they will need the furniture for.
❖ The weight and height of the furniture.
❖ Storage that is accessible for our pupils to select and access resources.
❖ The overall state of repair.
❖ The specific physical needs of our pupils and the modifications that they may require.

5. The furniture

Delving deeper	Where could you look?	Developing	Embedding	Secure	Our evidence – we know this because . . .
5.1 There are a range of seating types available that match the needs of the learners in the classroom.	• Environmental audits.				
5.2 Seating is at the correct height for the learner to access the table-top and have their feet flat on the floor.	• Environmental audits.				
5.3 Seating is of the correct weight for learners to be able to move them independently.	• Environmental audits.				
5.4 Tables are at the correct height for learners to access from their chairs comfortably.	• Environmental audits.				
5.5 The surfaces of table-tops are matt so that glare is reduced.	• Environmental audits.				
5.6 Tables do not move easily.	• Environmental audits.				
5.7 Storage promotes independent selection of and access to resources.	• Environmental audits.				

(Continued)

Delving deeper	Where could you look?	Developing	Embedding	Secure	Our evidence – we know this because . . .
5.8 Furniture is in a good state of repair and is safe for pupils to use.	• Environmental audits.				
5.9 Furniture location is flexible depending on the activity it is required for.	• Environmental audits. • Learning walks. • Lesson plans.				
5.10 Furniture can be moved according to the group size.	• Environmental audits. • Learning walks. • Lesson plans.				

6. Supporting Rules and Routines

Our rules and routines are needed to make sure that our schools run safely, smoothly and efficiently. They also promote a sense of safety and security as they limit anxiety and guesswork about what will happen, when it will happen and how it will happen. Pupils need an underpinning structure and a sense of familiarity as they continue to learn and develop, and classroom routines and procedures give students a predictable day. This is why classroom routines are important to the learning process.

Routines in the classroom make class time more enjoyable and productive. They offer students a sense of stability. By having classroom rules and procedures that everyone follows, pupils know our expectations. Communication of need via behaviour and distractions can decrease when students understand how to act.

Think about it – to get 30 pupils to all successfully move through the bathroom in preparation for lunchtime efficiently, well-embedded routines and rules are essential. Imagine the resulting chaos if it was a free-for-all!

Well-established rules and routines can:

❖ Create consistency: pupils learn what to expect when you are consistent. Routine consistency fosters a positive learning environment because the same rules apply to everyone so no one can be discriminated against or favoured.
❖ Enhance behaviour management: pupils learn rules and are clear about what is expected of them.
❖ Reduce classroom distractions: established routines support pupils in knowing what they are supposed to be doing, when and for how long. They can also support effective transitions from one activity to the next.
❖ Boost focus and engagement: pupils will become familiar with the classroom flow and what comes next, making it easier for them to focused and engaged.
❖ Create an effective classroom management plan.
❖ Make lesson planning easier: once you have a routine, it serves as an outline for lesson planning. It makes lesson planning easier and leaves more time for tailored teaching strategies because all you have to do is fill in the blanks based on the times you set for various subjects or activities.

Our environment can provide a conducive support to all of this.

6. Supporting rules and routines

Delving deeper	Where could you look?	Developing	Embedding	Secure	Our evidence – we know this because . . .
6.1 Our classroom rules are clearly displayed, supported with visual cues, positively phrased and understood by all.	• Environmental audits. • Learning walks. • Pupil voice activities.				
6.2 Pupils understand and observe classroom rules.	• Environmental audits. • Learning walks. • Pupil voice activities.				
6.3 We give positive and specific praise when pupils choose to follow classroom rules.	• Environmental audits. • Learning walks. • Pupil voice activities.				
6.4 Our rules are phrased in a way that is age- and developmentally-appropriate to the pupils in the classroom.	• Environmental audits. • Learning walks. • Pupil voice activities.				
6.5 Where appropriate, natural gesture and/ or signing is used to support the sharing of rules.	• Learning walks. • Pupil voice activities.				
6.6 Rules are consistent in expectation but flexible in practice.	• Learning walks. • Lesson observations. • Pupil voice activities. • School policy.				

(Continued)

Delving deeper	Where could you look?	Developing	Embedding	Secure	Our evidence – we know this because . . .
6.7 Clear routines are in place to support entry and exit to the classroom.	• Learning walks. • Lesson observations.				
6.7 Clear routines are in place to support transitions between lessons.	• Learning walks. • Lesson observations.				
6.8 Clear routines are in place to attract the attention of pupils.	• Learning Walks. • Lesson observations.				
6.9 Clear routines are in place to distribute and collect resources and learning materials.	• Learning walks. • Lesson observations.				
6.10 Additional time is given to those that need it to complete routines.	• Learning walks. • Lesson observations.				
6.11 Visual support (visual cues, signing and natural gesture) is used as appropriate to support the communication of routines.	• Lesson walks. • Learning observations.				
6.12 We give advance warning of changes in routines and rules is given.	• Lesson walks. • Learning observations.				

(Continued)

Delving deeper	Where could you look?	Developing	Embedding	Secure	Our evidence – we know this because . . .
6.13 There is a consistent approach in place for the routines for transitions so that pupils have: • Advance warning of changes to come. • Clear signals about when the transition will take place. • Reassurances about what is expected. • Visual support for who, what, where and when.	• Lesson walks. • Learning observations.				

7. Environmental Visual Supports

When we speak, the words we say disappear instantly. A visual support last for a much longer time, providing a potentially permanent record of information that we want to share. Visual supports may refer to items such as objects, photographs, signs and/or pictures used to aid and enhance communication and understanding. They are vital for pupils in that they can provide a long-lasting support to:

- ❖ Knowing and understanding what is to come.
- ❖ Know how long they might be doing something for.
- ❖ Know who they are working with.
- ❖ Understand when something might be happening.
- ❖ Where they will be going.
- ❖ Feel safe and secure.
- ❖ Have a reassuring resource that they can constantly check in with.
- ❖ Provide extra time to focus on and process information.
- ❖ Experience predictability and routine.
- ❖ Deal with change and transition – sudden and planned.
- ❖ Build independence.
- ❖ Understand information.
- ❖ Make choices.

Visual supports are often prioritised for pupils with communication and social, emotional and mental health needs. But in reality, we all rely on visuals to support us in our everyday life such as our diaries, information displays, checklists and signs. High- quality visual supports promote inclusion, as they are helpful for everyone.

7. Environmental visual supports

Delving deeper	Where could you look?	Developing	Embedding	Secure	Our evidence – we know this because . . .
7.1 Our classrooms contain visual timelines so that pupils know the lesson/event order from the start of the day until home time.	• Environmental audits. • Learning walks. • Pupil voice activities.				
7.2 Visual timelines are up to date.	• Environmental audits. • Learning walks.				
7.3 Visual timelines are displayed in a prominent place and can be seen clearly by all. Any laminating uses matt wallets to avoid glare.	• Environmental audits. • Learning walks.				
7.4 Our pupils know where the visual timelines in their classrooms are and can explain their purpose.	• Pupil Voice activities.				
7.5 Class rules and routines are supported with visual prompts (refer to section three for greater depth).	• Environmental audits. • Learning walks.				
7.6 For those that need it, visual supports are adapted such as: • Use of now/next boards. • Vertical checklists as opposed to picture- based horizontal timelines.	• Environmental audits. • Learning walks.				

(Continued)

Delving deeper	Where could you look?	Developing	Embedding	Secure	Our evidence – we know this because . . .
7.7 Task-slicing approaches are visually supported so that larger tasks are broken down into smaller tasks – each element can be seen and place keeping is supported.	• Environmental audits. • Learning walks.				
7.8 Resources are clearly labelled with words and pictures.	• Environmental audits. • Learning walks.				
7.9 Written words are supported with pictures and/or objects of reference to support understanding.	• Environmental audits. • Learning walks.				
7.10 A range of images are used to support communication of images such as: • Symbols. • Cartoon images. • Photographs. • Objects of reference.	• Environmental audits. • Learning walks.				

8. The Feeling

As stated at the start of this section, a magical classroom has a special sort of feeling to it. It is something that is difficult to describe and no checklist can account for it. Underpinning the feeling is what I believe to be a relational approach. One in which there is trust, nurture, acceptance, awareness and a mutual respect. One that acknowledges that everyone is valued for who they are.

Learning is risky – ultimately you have to be prepared to try something new and potentially fail. A relational approach puts relationships at the heart of teaching and emphasises the importance of meaningful connections between teachers and pupils, as well as between pupils and their peers. If there is a positive pupil–teacher relationship, then our pupils will be more inclined to be brave and take a risk.

It could be argued that underpinning values to this approach encompass:

- ❖ An ethos that is based around inclusive and compassionate approaches that benefit the well-being of all.
- ❖ The creation of a sense of belonging.
- ❖ Recognition of the gifts, talents and capacities of our pupils and their ability to achieve from their unique starting point.
- ❖ Child-centred approaches in which their voice is valued and central to planning.
- ❖ A high level of nurture which promotes a sense of safety and security.
- ❖ The recognition that behaviour is a method of communicating underlying needs.

If the learning environment can achieve this, then our pupils will feel safe and secure to take learning risks.

8. The feeling

Delving deeper	Where could you look?	Developing	Embedding	Secure	Our evidence – we know this because . . .
8.1 Our rules and routines are communicated clearly and supported with visual cues (for example: now and next boards).	• Environmental audits. • Learning walks.				
8.2 Tools are available for pupils to independently access to support self-regulation (for example: sensory tools).	• Environmental audits. • Learning walks. • Resource inventories.				
8.3 Our classrooms are well-ordered and organised.	• Environmental audits. • Learning walks.				
8.4 Positive affirmations are displayed in the classroom (for example: success boards, posters).	• Environmental audits. • Learning walks.				
8.5 A sense of belonging is encouraged (for example: photographs of the children, welcome signs).	• Environmental audits. • Learning walks. • Pupil voice activities.				
8.6 Displays are representative of the school community.	• Environmental audits. • Learning walks.				
8.7 Pupil achievement is displayed and celebrated.	• Environmental audits. • Learning walks.				
8.8 The environment fosters independence.	• School policy.				

(Continued)

8. The feeling

Delving deeper	Where could you look?	Developing	Embedding	Secure	Our evidence – we know this because . . .
8.1 Our rules and routines are communicated clearly and supported with visual cues (for example: now and next boards).	• Environmental audits. • Learning walks.				
8.2 Tools are available for pupils to independently access to support self-regulation (for example: sensory tools).	• Environmental audits. • Learning walks. • Resource inventories.				
8.3 Our classrooms are well-ordered and organised.	• Environmental audits. • Learning walks.				
8.4 Positive affirmations are displayed in the classroom (for example: success boards, posters).	• Environmental audits. • Learning walks.				
8.5 A sense of belonging is encouraged (for example: photographs of the children, welcome signs).	• Environmental audits. • Learning walks. • Pupil voice activities.				
8.6 Displays are representative of the school community.	• Environmental audits. • Learning walks.				
8.7 Pupil achievement is displayed and celebrated.	• Environmental audits. • Learning walks.				
8.8 The environment fosters independence.	• School policy.				

(Continued)

Delving deeper	Where could you look?	Developing	Embedding	Secure	Our evidence – we know this because . . .
8.9 Spaces to withdraw to are available for self-regulation.	• Environmental audits. • Learning walks. • Are the spaces visible and in use?				
8.10 Mistakes are valued and treated as opportunities for learning.	• Environmental audits. • Learning walks. • Pupil voice activities. • School policies.				
8.11 There is a high level of specific praise.	• Learning walks. • Lesson observations. • Pupil voice activities. • School policies.				
8.12 Transitions are carefully planned for.	• Lesson observations. • Learning walks. • Pupil voice activities. • School policies. • Transition plans. • Transition case studies.				
8.13 Our lesson plans take account of the pupil's unique starting point.	• Lesson plans. • Lesson observations.				
8.14 We actively seek pupil voice and act upon our findings.	• Pupil voice activities. • Pupil leadership activities.				
8.15 Our resources represent the school community.	• Pupil voice activities. • Resource inventories. • Lesson walks.				

Section Two
THE TOOLKIT

1. Meeting Sensory Needs

The following is a simple sensory environmental audit. It can be used to explore where you are at right now and what you may wish to work on to further develop your learning environments. This will lead to them becoming more effective in aiding your pupils to achieve a sensory balance for accessing learning. Remember, your local Occupational Therapy (OT) may be able to support you with this.

Environmental Sensory Audit Tool

What to look for	What we can see in our setting	What can we do to develop further?
Sight (visual)		
Lighting is regularly checked and changed if malfunctioning (for example: flickering).		
The impact of shadows cast by light sources is evaluated and altered if required.		
It is possible to alter lighting levels (for example: the offer of table-top lamps and use of blinds).		
Light reflecting from surfaces is minimised to avoid glare.		
Information and/or teaching staff are not directly in front of light sources.		
Sensory tools such as sunglasses and personalised light sources are available for pupils.		
Learning spaces are well organised and clutter free.		
The impact of display is carefully considered.		
There are designated spaces for work which gives clarity to organisation.		
Privacy boards are available to block out distractions.		
Visual high-interest resources are available (for example: 'Where's Wally?' puzzles).		
Hearing (auditory)		
Display screens, computers, audio systems, lights and other electrical items are switched off when not in use to avoid the sound of mains humming.		
Floors are carpeted to lessen noise created by the movement of people, chairs and desks.		
Doors and windows can be closed to limit background noise.		
Quiet spaces are available for pupils to withdraw to if needed.		
Sensory tools such as personalised noises (perhaps delivered via apps) and ear defenders are available.		
Acoustics are carefully considered and measures are in place to lessen echoes such as adding soft furnishings.		

(Continued)

What to look for	What we can see in our setting	What can we do to develop further?
Movement times in school are carefully considered so that noise is minimised by lessening crowding.		
Smell (olfactory)		
The smell of paints, glue, clay and cleaning fluids is minimised as far as possible (for example: consideration is given to storage.		
School staff recognise that personal smells (such as perfumes and deodorants) can distress some pupils.		
Environmental smells can be changed through air fresheners and smell diffusers.		
Alternative routes are available to miss out smells that pupils may find distressing such as avoiding the dining room and/or school kitchen.		
Careful consideration is given to the timing of the use of strong-smelling cleaning products.		
Touch (tactile)		
Alternative arrangements are made for pupils who find writing to be physically painful or difficult due to sensory challenges.		
Movement around school is timed carefully to avoid crowds.		
Queuing and lining up systems are carefully reviewed to allow for pupils' personal space.		
A range of tactile sensory tools are available for pupils to access.		
A range of seating modifications are available such as padding, cushions and throws are available.		
Modifications to school uniform are allowed (such as wearing a shirt untucked).		
Taste (gustatory)		
Staff do not insist upon meals being finished.		
Pupils are allowed to bring in alternative foods from home.		
Food is served on a variety of plates and/or in alternative containers to avoid food touching if required.		
Proprioception		
Weighted/pressure-based resources are available for pupils to access (for example: weighted blankets and lap pads).		
For those that need it, leaning is allowed.		
Designated work spaces are available for pupils who have difficulty with spatial awareness. If appropriate, pupils have increased work space.		
Furniture is at the correct height so that dangling legs are avoided.		
Interoception		
There is a designated place and a clear system/routine for pupils to follow if they feel they need to withdraw due to sensory overload to self-regulate.		

(Continued)

What to look for	What we can see in our setting	What can we do to develop further?
Vestibular		
Space is available for pupils to 'reset' via movement.		
Alternative seating is available to provide movement-based feedback (for example: wobble cushions, bouncy chairs).		
Apparatus and playground equipment provides opportunities for repetitive movements such as bouncing, spinning and swinging.		
Other considerations		
Classroom organisation and individual seating plans are flexible and take into consideration individual sensory concerns (for example: a pupil with a fascination with light reflection does not sit by the window).		
A low arousal space is available for pupils to withdraw to such as a blackout tent.		

Creating a Sensory Diet

It is not always possible for schools to provide a sensory room. For many pupils, sensory needs can be met successfully in the classroom via the provision of a sensory diet. A sensory diet follows the same principle as a food-based diet but is an activity diet containing sensory snacks. It is personalised to meet a pupil's sensory needs. Some activities can be used to 'perk up' pupils who may appear lethargic and others can calm pupils who may have large amounts of energy. Here are some ideas of tools that can be used within the environment to create a sensory experience or as resources that could go into a personalised sensory tool.

Sight	
Sensory avoiding	*Sensory seeking*
Cardboard tubes (to look through to block out visual stimuli)	Kaleidoscope
Plain fabric to drape over visually stimulating displays	*Where's Wally?* books
Cardboard with different-sized windows to look through	Fabric swatches containing small detailed patterns
Sunglasses	Magnifying glass
	Mirrors
	Mini torch
	Different-coloured overlays/acetate
	Things to spin and watch such as toy cars and airplanes (wheels and propellers)
Hearing	
Sensory avoiding	*Sensory seeking*
Ear defenders	Rain maker
Ear muffs	Percussion instruments
	Access to personal music devices/apps that play different sound effects

(Continued)

Smell	
Sensory avoiding	Sensory seeking
The opportunity to access preferred smells	Smell pots
	Herbs/spices
	Smell diffusers
Taste	
Sensory avoiding	Sensory seeking
Provide a range of tastes and textures to explore.	
Tactile	
Sensory avoiding	Sensory seeking
Gloves	Velcro
Alterations to school uniform	Soft, fluffy blankets
	Low grade sandpaper
	Velvet swatches
	Silk swatches
	Smooth pebbles
	Sequined fabric
	Different strengths of Theraputty

Don't forget to include opportunities to move to support the vestibular and proprioceptive sense. Ideas for this can include:

❖ Repetitive bouncing on a therapy/gym ball.
❖ Swinging.
❖ Opportunities to spin and rock.
❖ Weighted lap pads, blankets.
❖ Stretchy, tight fabric to wrap around the body and 'cocoon'.

Remember to think about how you will store these things. A large feely bag or inviting basket/box works well. You could also house these in a pop-up tent to create a sensory space.

A Sensory Profile: An Example in Practice

Here is a pupil's anonymised sensory profile that was developed in partnership with a school and the child to identify and support a pupil's sensory needs. We implemented the sensory diet aspect strategically to achieve the following:

❖ Offer a transition to learning activity to help the pupil achieve the right level of arousal to be ready to learn.

❖ Provide a sensory break during lessons as a valuable reset opportunity.
❖ To calm the pupil if they felt that they had too much energy to process and respond appropriately to instructions, information or learning tasks.

When the diet was fully implemented, we noted a 74% reduction in off-task behaviours.

My Sensory Profile

Name: Class:

Date completed:

	Experiences I enjoy	*Experiences I do not enjoy*
Hearing	Singing repetitive songs. Repeating polysyllabic words.	Loud, sudden noises. The hum from the computer.
Vision	Looking at lots of detail. Shiny things.	Bright light from the sun.
Smell	My dad's aftershave.	The smell in the toilets at school. The smell of the floor cleaner in the hall. The school kitchen smells like nasty cabbage!
Taste	Most foods.	Some spicy things like curry.
Tactile	My scarf and hoodie feel nice on my skin.	The labels in my trousers and pants. When other people are too close.
Proprioception	Heavy things on my lap and legs. Leaning on things.	When I can't 'find' my hands – they go all tingly and I have to squeeze them hard.
Vestibular	Swinging. Bouncing. Rocking. Twirling my head round and round fast. Spinning.	Feeling giddy when I haven't done spinning activities.

This is when I am more likely to seek sensory experiences and what it might look like.	*This is when I am more likely to avoid sensory experiences and what it might look like.*
• In maths when it is hard – like division. • When I am concentrating. • When teachers are talking to me for a long time. • When I think I might be in trouble. I rock, spin and twirl my head lots. I wriggle and make noises. I sit on my legs in a funny way so that I put my weight on them. I wrap myself up in my scarf.	• When I am sad. • When I am tired. • When I am worrying about something. I go away on my own where there are fewer people. I put my head on the desk and cover my eyes. I make my own noises – usually singing. I am jumpy.

These are places in school where I am 'just right' and why.	These are places in school where I might need help to manage my senses and why. This is what good help looks like.
The dark den tent. When I can sit at the back on my own desk. In Mrs XXXX's office – it is quiet there. I like the music room – it is darker and there are sounds I like.	The dining room – too loud, busy and smelly. In the school hall – too smelly and too many people clapping in assemblies. The entrance hall – too busy with the people coming in and out and the door buzzer makes me jump.

My Sensory Diet			
	Perk Up	**Just Right**	**Calming**
Hearing	• Singing	• Use of ear defenders	• Singing • Whispering my favourite words.
Vision	• *Where's Wally?* book for five minutes. • Looking at my favourite fabric samples for five minutes.	• Sitting at the back of the classroom where it is a bit darker – away from the windows.	• Five minutes looking through my kaleidoscope.
Smell	• Sit by the smell diffuser when we have orange and lemon oil in it.	• Sit by the smell diffuser when we have the lavender oil in it.	• Spray my dad's aftershave onto my wrist and have a big sniff.
Taste	• Nothing needed.	• Nothing spicy!	• Nothing needed.
Tactile	• Use my rough fidget tools and stroke them lots.	• Avoid busy spaces.	• Stroke my scarf and wrap it around my neck. • Wear my hoodie and stroke the sleeves on my face. • My velvet fidget tool.
Proprioception	• Press-ups. • Move a heavy object (dragging and pushing). • Play 'Row, Row, Row, Your Boat' with a partner.	• Weighted lap pad. • Weighed blanket.	• Lean against the wall. • Self-massage.
Vestibular	• Swinging fast and high. • Rocking. • Bouncing. • Spinning around.	• Sit on the gym ball and gently bounce while I am working.	• Yoga poses – especially where my head is upside- down. • A turn in the rocking chair.

2. Display

There are several different approaches that can be taken to classroom display. This has been backed up by research that suggested that children learn more effectively when extraneous details are removed. This has also been found to be the case for reduced 'visual noise' in the classroom. The first tool sets out some useful reminders for display that can be shared with your colleagues:

Principles for Display:

1. Offer a distraction-free stage – as the teacher, you need to draw in the attention of your pupils. The space you teach from should be the barest part of the room. Displays that could potentially distract from the lesson at hand should be outside of your pupils' field of vision. Busier displays can be at the sides and rear of the classroom.

2. Less is more – aim to make your classroom feel and look inviting using as few elements as possible.

3. Learning from displays goes from the walls into the head, so remember that learning refers to what goes on in our heads, not what goes on the wall. Remove scaffolds that have become redundant, out of date, secure in the pupils' learning bank or that interfere with retrieval practice. When you are asking review questions, once secure with their knowledge, ask your pupils to search their memory, not turn and look at a display.

4. Contextual display – if a visual scaffold is required for a particular subject or activity, don't display it until you need to refer to it.

5. Design your displays with clarity in mind – cut out redundant information, organise information into meaningful chunks/sections, align elements for easy visual navigation and resist the temptation to use complicated and overly fancy fonts and colour schemes.

6. Make your displays easy to navigate – use colour coding and grouping to pull connected information together. Use headings and keep things well spaced. Place boxes/borders around the key information so that it is clearly signposted. Select a consistent font and colour scheme.

Top Tips for Increasing the Accessibility of Your Displays

❖ Add a voice-recording device such as a Talking Tin or recordable postcard and record key information or processes. Pupils can visit the display and play the information whilst looking at it.

❖ If display items need laminating for longevity, use matt laminates as opposed to gloss. This will limit glare.

❖ Consider the size of display items carefully. Can everything be seen and read clearly from all seating positions in the room?

❖ Add real objects and texture to support understanding of subject specific and descriptive vocabulary. For example, to support the word 'rough' – the letters could be cut out of sandpaper or a rough piece of tree bark displayed next to it.

❖ Consider font choices carefully. Stick to one consistent style. Sans serif fonts such as Arial and Comic Sans can help lettering appear less crowded.

❖ Use bold for emphasis but avoid use of italics and underlining as this can make text appear to run together and appear crowded.

❖ To aid navigation, aim for headings to be 20% bigger that the rest of the text.

❖ Use single colour backgrounds.

❖ Avoid green, red and pink as these colours can be difficult for those with colour-vision deficiencies.

❖ Make sure there is a good contrast between the text and the background – aim for a dark-coloured print on a pastel background.

❖ Explore the use of bullet points and or numbering.

❖ Colour-code and group linked information.

3. Access to Resources that Support Learning

Coming up is a menu of resources that can be used to support pupils across the four broad areas of need as identified in the 2015 SEND Code of Practice. It isn't an exhaustive list but will provide you with some ideas as a useful starting point. Before you gather all of your resources together, here are some of the topics and some answers that I often discuss with teachers and support staff.

Resources: Some Things to Consider

Where will the resources be stored?

Consider:

❖ Are the resources best placed on individual tables or in a centralised area of the classroom.

❖ How freely do you want the pupils to access the resources provided?

❖ How will you label them – words, symbols and/or photographs are all options?

What can I do to encourage pupils who are reluctant to use additional supportive resources?

1. Model using them yourself as part of your everyday practice. When you do make it clear how that resource can help – make the benefits obvious.

2. Leave the resources out for all to use – this is inclusive and will help pupils feel no different to anyone else. The resources are for everyone!

The pupils don't seem to use them.

Have they been explicitly taught how and when to use them? It is good practice to introduce one resource at a time making it clear:

1. What the resource is.
2. When you might use it.
3. How you use it – use adult and peer models.

Praise the pupil for using the resource using explicit language the links their work to the resource.

How can I make sure that pupils select the right resource for the job?

Challenge pupils in a supportive way by asking them what resource they have selected, why they have selected it and how they are going to use the resource. You could also complete resource-matching conversations in which you explore what the problem is and what could help. Some schools like to have a suggested resource element to their subject-specific displays.

Resource Menu	
Cognition and Learning	*Communication and Interaction*
• Task checklists (visual and or written). • Now/next boards to aid with planning. • Voice recording devices to aid with 'holding' information. • Task-slicing boards. • Number lines and 100 squares. • Concrete apparatus (such as cubes and Dienes) to support number work. • Phonic choice charts to aid spelling. • Alphabet strips. • Mini dry-wipe boards and dry-wipe pens for jottings. • Resources that can be used as a discreet 'help needed' signal. • Dictionaries (including picture, word-based and spelling support). • Sentence starters. • Model writing frames/graphic organisers.	• Aided Language Displays to help with choosing, teaching new vocabulary and using new language functions such as making a request. • Visual timelines. • Objects of reference. • Personalised vocabulary books. • Word webs. • Sensory tools to aid concentration (see previous sensory ideas linked to the environment). • Voice recording devices so that key words and instructions can be played back. • Word mats – subject specific key vocabulary with supporting pictures.
Social, Emotional and Mental Health	*Physical and/or Sensory*
• Visual supports to show and describe emotions. • Check-in devices so that pupils can show how they are feeling. • Sensory tools. • A place to store worries for adults to check and support (such as a worry box or worry monster). • Personalised journals.	• Seating wedge. • Writing slope. • A range of pencil grips. • Adapted scissors. • Coloured overlays. • Rulers, protractors and other tools with handles. • Anti-slip mats or non-slip silicone roll. • Magnifying devices. • Voice-recording devices. • Wobble cushion. • Chunky writing and mark-making tools. • Triangular/easy grip writing and mark making tools. • Lightweight tools for writing and other classroom tasks.

An Example in Practice – The Help Yourself Shelf

The 'help yourself shelf' was implemented for a class whose teacher felt had become 'learned helpless'. The class teacher had identified that her class constantly came to her for support and reassurance as opposed to trying to independently problem solve first. To support with this issue we set up a central store of support resources which could be accessed by her pupils as and when needed. The crucial rule here was that the adults in the room could only be asked for help after the pupils had exhausted what was available on the 'help yourself shelf' first.

The resources selected came from two different sources – the menu of resources provided matched to the four broad areas of need (these were ordinarily and always available) and some subject-specific supports that could be changed according to the topic.

To give you an idea, here is the list of items from the classroom 'help yourself shelf' that were available for a lesson in which the pupils were building and testing electrical circuits.

Ordinarily Available Resources	Subject-Specific Resources
• Voice-recording devices. • Coloured overlays. • Dictionaries (word-based and picture-based). • Task-slicing boards. • Mini dry-wipe whiteboards and pens. • Phonic choice charts. • Number lines and 100 squares. • Sensory tools. • Easy grip and lightweight writing tools. • Pencil grips. • Non-slip matting.	• Additional batteries, wires and bulbs. • A recount-based writing frame to support the recording of the pupils' investigations. • An electricity-specific word mat. • An example of a working electrical circuit. • Linked textbooks with key pages/information signposted with sticky notes. • Voice-recording devices with task instructions pre-recorded.

In addition to all of this, the class teacher had provided additional stationery such as spare pencils, rulers, rubbers and pencil sharpeners.

When observing the class, I noted that:

❖ All pupils were happy to go and fetch what they needed when they needed it with independence.

❖ Those that required additional support made good use of the 'help yourself shelf' before they approached their teacher.

❖ The teacher was able to concentrate more on supporting pupils with developing their subject knowledge and probing deeper as opposed to firefighting issues.

The benefits

Over time the class teacher felt that her pupils had:

- ❖ Become more independent as they tried to support themselves first before seeking additional adult support.
- ❖ Grown in resilience as they became more willing to try more than one way of supporting themselves when something was unsuccessful.
- ❖ Learnt to become more considered in their choices of support resource as they explored the options available.
- ❖ Become less self-conscious about using resources and appearing different from their peers as everything is available to everyone.
- ❖ Become more aware of what works well for them as they developed resource preferences.
- ❖ Become more aware of when they 'were stuck'.

There are lots of different names for 'help yourself shelves'. You might like:

- ❖ The Stuck Solver Station.
- ❖ The Enable Table.
- ❖ Solve It Yourself Station.

4. Supporting Pupils Who Are Hearing and/or Visually Impaired

Hearing-impaired pupils find it difficult to filter sounds, so any background noise is going to get mixed in with what they are trying to listen to and make understanding speech more challenging. For example, if they wear hearing aids or implants, it makes all sounds in that room louder. Therefore, it is essential to create an environment that is conducive to good listening so that your pupils have the optimal learning conditions to access sound in order to develop their listening and language skills. This will not only support hearing-impaired pupils – it is good for everyone. Here are a few pointers:

Creating Good Listening Conditions – Checklist

Good Listening Condition Indicators	In Place	To Develop
Background noise is limited as far as possible (for example: doors and windows are closed).		
Soft furnishings and carpet are used to lessen noises and echoes.		
The teacher is face-on to the pupils so that facial expressions, gestures and lips can clearly be seen.		
Seating arrangements are flexible so that pupils can move to a place in the classroom that optimises their ability to hear and see the teacher.		
Visual cues such as signing, Makaton, natural gesture, photographs and symbols are used to aid understanding.		
Pupils are not required to listen for too long.		
Talk is kept to an appropriate pace.		
Pupils are encouraged to signal and seek support if they have not heard or have not understood.		
The teacher frequently questions to check that pupils have comprehended what has been said.		
Pupils remain in the classroom so that they have opportunities to access incidental learning opportunities.		
Lighting sources are adequate so that the teacher, peers and teaching resources can be seen clearly.		
The person that the pupils need to attend to is not stood in front of a light source.		
'Visual noise' such as cluttered displays is reduced so that the pupil can attend to the main source of information.		
The class teacher ensures that everyone is attending before beginning to speak.		

Positive Learning Conditions for Visually Impaired Pupils – Checklist

Positive Learning Conditions for Visually Impaired Pupils Indicators	In Place	To Develop
The class teacher avoids standing in front of light sources.		
Seating arrangements are flexible so that the learner can move to the position that works best for them to be able to see resources.		
Individual copies of notes and teaching materials are provided and appropriately modified.		
A clearly contrasting pen is used on a clean writing surface for demonstrations.		
Resources are produced on appropriately coloured paper and enlarged to match the pupils' needs.		
Real objects and artefacts are used to support learning.		
Brightness of lighting can be altered.		
Blackout blinds are available.		
PE equipment is clean and creates a good contrast (for example: green beanbags/ balls are not used on grass).		
Walkways are clear.		
Furniture does not create obstacles.		
The layout of the classroom remains consistent.		
Steps and changes in the gradient of flooring are clearly demarcated.		
Glare from surfaces is limited.		
Pupils have access to power sources for their electronic equipment of required.		
Classroom labels are clearly written and produced at an appropriate size for viewing.		

5. The Furniture

To promote inclusivity, classrooms can incorporate furniture designs and adaptations that cater for a wide variety of needs and preferences. For example, adjustable desks and chairs can accommodate students with differing physical requirements, allowing them to find the most comfortable position for learning. In addition, furniture can be arranged to create open spaces that facilitate movement and collaboration, enabling students to engage with each other and their surroundings more effectively. Many flexible options are now available when thinking about the most effective furniture for meeting your pupils' needs, in order to create the best possible conditions for comfort and learning. Here are some things to consider.

Furniture Element	To Consider
Seating	• Is it an appropriate height for the pupil? • Do pupils' feet connect with the floor? • Can pupils independently move their chairs. • Is the shape appropriately contoured for comfort? • Is additional padding available for comfort? • For those that require it are sensory needs accounted for such as features that provide rocking and bouncing? • Are there a range of alternatives to conventional seating available such as beanbags and large cushions? • Can you provide different-coloured chairs to aid the giving of instructions (for example: 'Everyone on the red table....') and to aid with group identification? • Are seats strong, durable and easy to clean?
Tables	• Are tables of an adjustable height? • Can they be repositioned easily? • Are the surfaces matt to limit glare? • Can you provide different-coloured tables to aid the giving of instructions (for example: 'Everyone on the red table....') and to aid with group identification? • Are seats strong, durable and easy to clean?
Storage	• Are there a range of modification options available so that clutter can be minimised but key resources are on display to aid accessibility and independence of access? • Are surfaces matt to limit glare? • Are the items stored at a height that is accessible to pupils? • Are storage compartments labelled with text and supporting images so that pupils can find what they would like with ease? • Are storage units strong, durable and easy to clean? • Are personalised storage options available for those that need them?
Learning Support Resources	• Are the heights of resources such as Tuff Trays, sand and water trays and easels adjustable? • Are they easy to move to allow for flexibility of where activities are completed? • Are they strong, durable and easy to clean?

6. Supporting Rules and Routines

What are rules and routines?

It is important to establish the difference between rules and routines.

❖ Rules are something that we all must do or follow.
❖ Routines are the usual order or usual way that we carry out a task.

Once everyone is clear on this, a useful place to start is with what your pupils think. After all, the rules and routines in place for your classroom directly impact upon them in terms of their:

❖ Understanding of expectations.
❖ Feelings of safety and security.
❖ Levels of anxiety.
❖ Understanding of what is happening.
❖ Feeling part of a team – a sense of belonging.

Here is a pupil voice activity that you can complete to work out if your rules and routines are perceived appropriately by your pupils.

Finding Out About Our Rules and Routines

What do you think about . . .	Please colour the box that you agree with.		
1. I know what the school rules are.	✓	?	X
2. I know what my classroom rules are.	✓	?	X
3. I know where the rules are displayed.			
4. I can read my classroom rules.	✓	?	X
5. I can see pictures that help me understand the rules.	✓	?	X
6. I feel safe in school.	✓	?	X
7. I am helped to understand what is going to happen and when it will happen.	✓	?	X
8. The rules are used fairly.	✓	?	X
9. I do not worry about changes when they happen.	✓	?	X
10. The teachers warn us before changes happen.	✓	?	X
11. There is a timer that shows us when a change will happen.	✓	?	X
12. Pictures are used to show us the order that things happen in.	✓	?	X
13. We can join in with helping to write our school and classroom rules.	✓	?	X
14. We can join in with helping to decide what the routines should be.	✓	?	X
15. I can ask for help if I do not understand the rules and routines.	✓	?	X

Do you want to tell us anything else about rules and routines in school?

Creating the Rules – Some Helpful Hints

Co-production

Working to establish classroom rules in partnership with your pupils is essential. This will provide them with greater ownership and make the rules more meaningful and relevant to them. If your pupils 'buy in' then they are more likely to follow them.

Keep it short and keep it simple!

Avoid long lists of rules with complicated language. Keeping the rules short and simple makes them more memorable and easy to refer to. We are much more likely to mention them specifically when praising or reminding.

Focus on the positive

Phrase your rules in a positive way. This will push your pupils to focus upon what you all agree you want to see and focus upon what can be done as opposed to avoiding what can't.

Make them accessible

Can your written rules be supported with visual images that show what you want to see? Could you have voice-recording devices with the rules recorded on as part of your positive display so that pupil can play them back to listen.

Keep referring back to them

Regularly remind pupils of the rules and encourage them to remind each other. Refer to them when praising them and thanking them for positive behaviours. For example: 'Well done and thank you for following our class rule that says . . . Your choice means that. . . .'

Make links back to learning

Link rules back to learning so that pupils understand the benefits of them and how they contribute to a positive learning environment.

Be adaptive

Change and adapt the rules as your classes or the school changes.

Be consistent in principles but flexible in practice

For many reasons, rules can be broken. It is important that we are always looking at the individual student and their circumstances in order to support them effectively.

Remember

Having clear boundaries is essential and consistency within a school is key. Rules can be positive and they can support pupils in making progress. However, if they are just stuck on a wall and are not part of our pupils' learning journey and everyday experiences, then they are redundant.

Rules: An Example in Practice

Here is an example of some positive, simple and short rules from a Year Two classroom that the pupils find easy and effective to follow.

We want our classroom to be a happy place where we can all learn. That is why we have all agreed to try to:

1. Use kind words to talk to each other.
2. Be ready to learn.
3. Follow instructions the first time.

For each rule there is a photograph that shows the children from the class demonstrating the expectation. There is also a voice recording device containing a recording of a pupil reading out the rule. This is displayed next to each rule.

All children have placed their handprint around the rules to show that they 'have a hand' in co-producing the rules and that they agree to do their best to try and follow them.

When I asked one of the pupils about the rules they told me that:

'I like our rules. They are easy to remember and help us all know what to do so that the classroom is happy and full of learning. If you do the rules you can get praised. That feels nice!'

Top Tips for Establishing and Supporting Routines

1. Keep routines simple. Aim for the minimum number of steps to complete a task.
2. Provide visual supports so that pupils with language difficulties can see what to do rather than relying upon written or spoken language. This will help make them tangible. Support your routines with natural gestures or signing.
3. Display routines in the classroom using posters and lots of visual supports.
4. Model them consistently and point out pupils that are following classroom routines effectively. Praise pupils specifically spelling out precisely which element of the routine they followed and how this helped everyone – link this back to learning.
5. Encourage pupils to have a say in what routines they would like to develop and what might work well for them. This may make them more inclined to follow your classroom routines.
6. Warn pupils of changes in routines in advance.
7. Teach all classroom routines explicitly.

Here are some examples of visual supports that can be used to support pupils in following routines.

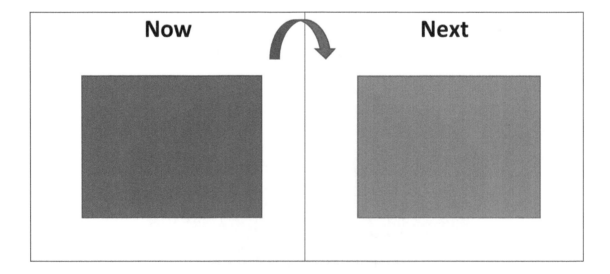

Images of the activities can be placed in the appropriate box. Pupils can be encouraged to update their now/next board.

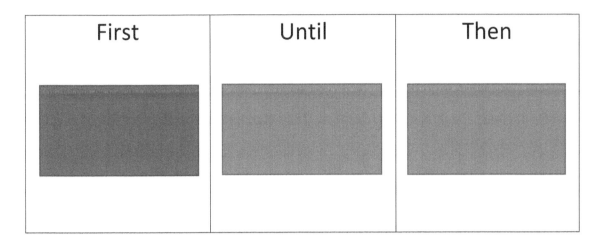

First	Until	Then

This resource moves the now/next board on a gear so that pupils can work towards being less prompt dependent. The 'until' section can support by helping them to know how long and activity will take or what finished looks like meaning that they can make a more independent transition. You might wish to give them the choice about the until section. This could link to a feeling. For example: 'First, I will play with the sand until I feel thirsty. Then I will have a drink.'

The now/next board and first/until/then board can be further extended with additional steps added into a routine.

7. Environmental Visual Supports

In creating visual supports for your learning environment, the most important thing is to choose those that work the most effectively for the pupils that you are working with. Consideration needs to be given to ensuring that your chosen visuals are easy to understand, clear, and interesting to look at. They also need to be easy for you to produce and use in your setting.

The first tool considers how to make and then implement a visual timeline.

Making and Using a Visual Timeline

There are commercially available visual timelines, schedules or frameworks available to purchase. However, it is often best to produce your own, as it can be personalised to your class and school and also tailored to meet the needs of your pupils.

Key points to consider:

❖ Consider the size of the step, activity or lesson to be represented by the timeline. (For example: for getting dressed for PE, you would need to include a picture representing each item of clothing the pupils will take off and then put on in the correct order.)

❖ The timeline will need to show the order of activities, steps in a task or order of lessons from left to right or from top to bottom. This format will need to be consistently stuck to. It is important to ensure that the pictures are displayed in the correct order.

❖ Consider the type of visual representation you will use. When deciding this, consider carefully the understanding and developmental level of your pupils and match the visual carefully to their unique starting point. This may mean use of symbols, photographs or more representational pictures.

❖ Consider how you can show which activity, step or lesson the pupil is currently doing. For example: a star or arrow that can be moved along the timeline as you move through the activities. Alternatively, each individual activity, step or lesson could be removed from the timeline once it is completed. You could use a 'door' or flap that could be closed over the activity to hide it in order to indicate that it is complete.

❖ Make sure that the visual timeline is located in a place easily seen by the pupils.

❖ Consider progression. You may want to start with now/next and then build up the number of elements included. You may also want to move from objects to photographs to more representational images.

How do I use a visual timeline?

The visual timeline is an interactive tool and is only useful when it is used in this way. To help your pupils to know where they are in the day, the visual timeline needs to be referred to regularly so that it is always up to date. There also needs to be a visual reminder of what has already happened and of what is yet to happen. This needs to be designed for the pupils to spot at a glance. Often, school staff find that encouraging the pupils to take ownership and responsibility for the class timeline is the most effective way of doing this.

Step one: introduce the visual timeline to the pupils at the start of the activity, lesson or time period that it relates to. For example, at the beginning of the day, show the pupils the lessons that will be taking place in the morning. If there is a choosing activity, make sure that there is a picture which represents 'choosing time'.

Step two: carry out the activity or step that is first on the visual timeline, referring to the visual timeline as you go.

Step three: refer back to the visual timeline making it explicit that this activity has been completed. Show this using your preferred method.

Task slicing refers to the act of looking at a completed task – the end game – and then breaking this down into the smaller, more manageable steps that will achieve this. 'Mini motivators' can be included between each step, with a larger reward included at the end. Timers can also be used to support the completion of each stage. Task slicing is particularly effective for pupils who may experience difficulties with task organisation, maintenance and completion. It is often helpful to represent a task-slicing approach using a visual support.

Task Slicing – An Example in Practice

One of the recommendations I made in a pupil's report stated the following:

❖ The pupil would benefit from a task-slicing approach to support them in developing appropriate task organisation, execution, maintenance and completion skills. This will support them to work with greater independence in the classroom. The task-slicing approach should be visually supported to aid understanding, place-keeping and productivity.

From this recommendation the following visual was developed and implemented in a Science lesson:

I need to: make a diagram that explains the water cycle in the correct order.					
Step One		*Step Two*		*Step Three*	*Finished*
Cut out all of the pictures and words.		Put them in the right order in my book.		Check that they are right and stick them in.	
Five minutes		Five minutes		Five minutes	
Images designed by FreePik					

This visual was created as a template on a mini dry-wipe board and the pupil, with some support from staff, was able to draw the task elements in the relevant section. Motivators and the end 'prize' were pre-agreed.

The class teacher noted that there was a huge improvement in the pupil's ability to complete a task with greater independence. They also noted that the pupil's work was much more likely to stay within the topic boundaries.

Top Tips for the Effective use of Visuals

❖ The most effective way to use the visual support provided needs to be explicitly taught. Introduce the visual to pupils and explain what you are going to be using it for. Model how to use it making the invisible visible. For example: 'I need to know what lesson is next so that I have the right equipment ready. I'm going to check on our visual timeline.'

❖ Carefully consider when and where you will be using the visual. In what activities and/or situations would it be the most useful? Link this to the best place to display it for ease of access and relevance.

❖ If you are using objects, they need to be meaningful and motivating for the pupils. You can start to use photos/pictures alongside the object to support pupils to transition from object to picture recognition.

❖ Be consistent in your use of visuals. Your pupils need to see visuals lots of times to begin to understand their use. Make certain that you use the same visual for the same thing.

❖ Make sure the visuals are clearly visible to all pupils from all locations. They need to be of an appropriate size, printed with appropriate colour and contrast choices with limited glare.

❖ Make your visuals accessible to all supporting the pupils. For example: have a specific area for keeping objects and symbols and make sure everyone knows where it is, or, if using a tablet device, put a shortcut on the home screen.

8. The Feeling

As stated earlier in this section, we are aiming for a classroom that enables all children to feel safe and secure, because learning is risky. What if we fail? Therefore, we are working towards establishing an environment that:

❖ Is inclusive and compassionate with approaches that benefit the well-being of all.
❖ Is conducive to the creation of a sense of belonging.
❖ Recognises the gifts, talents and capacities of all pupils and their ability to achieve from their unique starting point.
❖ Deploys child-centred approaches in which their voice is valued and central to planning.
❖ Nurtures all to promote a sense of safety and security.
❖ Recognises that behaviour is a method of communicating underlying needs.

Therefore, a relational approach is vital. The starting point for this is to consider the six underlying principles of nurture.

Nurture Checklist

Principle One: Children's Understanding Is Understood Developmentally

❖ All teaching staff are able to identify and know the unique starting point of their pupils.
❖ Lessons are adapted to match learning and developmental needs.
❖ Pupils' development is carefully tracked and analysed. The findings are acted upon to modify teaching and learning strategies.
❖ Appropriate scaffolds are provided so that pupils can access learning as independently as possible.
❖ Staff have a sound knowledge of child development milestones.
❖ Expectations for learners are age- and ability-appropriate.
❖ There are high expectations in place for all.
❖ Tasks are adapted around social and emotional competence as well as around curricular ability, for example, children and young people who have difficulties working with others on tasks are grouped with other children and young people who can give support or are given adult support and guidance on working with others.
❖ There is a clear balance between support and challenge within the curriculum; for example, pupils are given work that they are comfortable doing alongside some tasks that may be more challenging. Adults mediate this learning and provide a safe base for learners when learning is more challenging.
❖ Pupils are given choices about the mode of learning they engage in, for example, active or passive, cooperative or individual.

❖ There are opportunities for play-based learning dependent on the developmental level of the pupils.

❖ Staff have an awareness of language development and modify the language they use depending on the need of the children and young people.

❖ The language used by the teachers in the classroom suits the developmental needs of the pupils; for example, instructions are broken down and understanding checked.

❖ Individualised targets are set for children and young people where appropriate – pupils are aware of these and they are either reinforced orally or in a visual or recorded way.

Principle Two: The Classroom Offers a Safe Base

❖ There are clear routines and systems visible in the classroom, for example, welcome, check-ins, review of lesson.

❖ Clear and consistent expectations and boundaries are set within the class – orally, visually, written.

❖ The classroom has designated safe areas that children and young people can go to if they find the general classroom areas overwhelming or challenging. Children and young people have a choice in how they use these areas.

❖ There is a clear behaviour/relational policy which staff follow to ensure that reactions and expectations are consistent from all.

❖ Consistent de-escalation strategies are in use.

❖ Positive relationships are modelled.

❖ Staff consult with children and young people when there are changes to the routine.

❖ Appropriate adult support and structure is provided to children and young people who need it; for example, adults stay closer to children and young people in class who may need regular checking in and feedback.

❖ The language used by staff in the classroom clearly communicates to pupils that they are welcome and will be supported to achieve and feel safe and happy within the learning environment.

❖ Staff make good use of positive relationships to help encourage and guide pupils in appropriate behaviour and avoid an over-reliance on rewards and punishments as a way of managing or controlling behaviour.

Principle Three: The Importance of Nurture for the Development of Well-Being

❖ Staff are warm and welcoming.

❖ Taking a learning risk is encouraged and celebrated.

❖ Positive relationships are embedded and support pupils to intrinsically make positive choices.

❖ Staff acknowledge pupils' achievements and challenges by commenting on what they have done rather than any personal characteristic of the pupil which they may find difficult to accept.

❖ An appropriate level of support and challenge is in place.

❖ A growth mind-set is prompted in helping pupils to see that they can achieve things by effort and perseverance.

❖ There is explicit teaching of social and emotional skills within the classroom according to the stage and developmental needs of the children and young people. For example, turn-taking and negotiating.

Principle Four: Language Is Vital as a Means for Communication

❖ Staff provide running commentaries on what the pupil is doing and thinking to help them make sense of the world around them.

❖ Staff recognise that pupils need opportunities to practise the skills needed for self-awareness, self-management, social awareness and relationship management and support pupils in developing these skills.

❖ Staff do not assume that children and young people understand the language of emotion and help to scaffold their understanding of this.

❖ Pupils' unique language levels are understood and appropriately catered for.

❖ Where appropriate, specialist advice is sought from a speech and language therapist.

❖ Staff understand language development milestones and can recognise when a pupil's language may not be developing typically.

Principle Five: All Behaviour Is Communication

❖ Staff demonstrate their understanding of the fact that behaviour is communication. For example, they give the opportunity for the pupil to explain what has happened – either at the time when appropriate or after a situation has occurred.

❖ Behaviours that are expected within the classroom are explicitly named and modelled by staff. For example, listening, sharing and helping others.

❖ There is explicit teaching of social and emotional skills within the classroom according to the stage and developmental needs of the children and young people; for example, turn-taking, negotiating.

❖ Staff either guide pupils to seek out self-regulation activities or allow pupils the choice to seek this out for themselves.

- ❖ Staff recognise that pupils may be unable to comply with external rewards and reinforcements so support them to comply with requests, for example, 'I see you need help with. . .'.
- ❖ Staff are able to stay calm and patient when pupils are distressed to help them feel emotionally contained when their feelings are overwhelming.
- ❖ Where any consequences are applied to behaviour, these are fair, proportionate and logical.
- ❖ Staff support conflict resolution by giving pupils the opportunity to find their way back from situations. Pupils are also supported by staff coaching them in how to step back from a situation.
- ❖ Restorative conversations and language are used when incidents occur. For example, what happened, what were you thinking at the time?

Principle Six: The Importance of Transitions in Children's Lives

- ❖ There are clear plans for the day in the classroom which helps children and young people to know what is coming up.
- ❖ There are clear routines visible in the classroom, for example, welcome, check-ins, ending of lessons.
- ❖ Plans for transitions between key stages and joining/leaving school are made and personalised.
- ❖ Information about pupils is shared appropriately and in advance to other professionals.
- ❖ For some pupils, early transitions are planned and actioned.
- ❖ Transition routines are supported visually.
- ❖ Pupils have a clear idea of what will be happening, when and for how long.
- ❖ Endings and what 'finished' looks like are explicitly explained so that pupils know what they are aiming for.

Part of creating the feeling is having pupils who are able to self-monitor and regulate. Self-monitoring is checking in with yourself so that you can recognise how you are and how you are feeling. Self-regulation involves acting upon your findings from self-monitoring and then responding in order to control your own feelings, emotions and behaviour. They both require the ability to pay attention to relevant stimuli and then respond accordingly. This is where the following tool can be helpful. Here is an example to support you in practice:

Self-Monitoring and Regulation – An Example in Practice

Here is an example of a self-monitoring and regulation chart developed and used by a pupil to work out how he was feeling and what strategies could be used to self-regulate.

	Looks like	Feels like	I can	You can
Not Okay	Hiding under the table Rocking Shouting	Hot Funny tummy Sweaty My face feels red	Go to the dark den by myself. Move to the corridor and read my book. Show my red card. Punch the pillow in the dark den.	Give me time and space. Remind me I can go to the dark den. Give me my sensory toolbox.
Changing	Fidgety Don't care (I do)	Ants crawling on me	Show my timeout card. Ask to get a drink. Tell a friend that I don't feel right. Ask for some help from a grown up. Use my sensory toolbox.	Ask me if I am okay. Listen carefully to me. Remind me to get a drink. Distract me with colouring or a puzzle book.
Okay	Happy Doing my work Joining in Peopling	All good!	Enjoy it! Record what I did in my celebration book and share with my special adult.	Praise me. Let me enjoy it.

Top Tips for Creating the Feeling

1. Show the pupils that you have held them in mind. This means showing the pupil that you have thought about them when they were not with you. For example: 'I saw that your favourite football team won on Saturday. I thought of you.'

2. Demonstrate unconditional positive regard. Unconditional positive regard is a stance that communicates the following message to your pupils: I care about you. You have value. You don't have to do anything to prove it to me, and *nothing is going to change my mind.*

3. Keep open and welcoming body language.

4. Use positive language and keep praise specific. Tell the pupils what they are doing well and thank them for it.

5. Celebrate wonky work. This is about celebrating the pupil's mistakes that have led to learning – the journey, not the outcome.

6. Be dependably real and predictably boring so that pupils know where they stand and what to expect from you. This provides safety.

7. Teach routines for the promotion of security.

8. Ask for, value and act upon pupil voice.

9. Take an interest – what do your pupils like? What are their hobbies and interests?

10. Encourage belonging – include photographs of the pupils in the classroom and personal significant objects.

Section Three

TEACHING AND LEARNING

High-Quality Adaptive Teaching

The concept of adaptive teaching appears in the Early Career Teacher Framework (Department for Education, 2019). It states that Early Career Teachers should:

Provide opportunity for all pupils to experience success by:

- Adapting lessons, whilst maintaining high expectations for all, so that all pupils have the opportunity to meet expectations.
- Balancing input of new content so that pupils master important concepts.
- Making effective use of teaching assistants.

(ECT Framework, 2019 – Standard 5 Adapting Teaching)

It is also a feature of Teacher Standard 5, which refers to knowing when to differentiate appropriately, understanding the factors that can inhibit learning, being aware of child development and understanding the needs of all pupils.

In day-to-day classroom practice this can mean continuously assessing the strengths and needs of all learners and adapting the pedagogy accordingly. Often, this can be in the moment as a result of your formative assessment. So, for example, whilst teaching your careful questioning of pupils may reveal that thy have misunderstood a concept such as the differences between acute and obtuse angles. Rather than continuing, you might adapt your

DOI: 10.4324/9781032643076-6

approach and reteach the concept in a different way to ensure that pupils are secure before moving on. This could be achieved by revisiting and demonstrating using an alternative resource or allowing pupils to complete further worked examples before independent practice.

In making adaptions to our teaching it is important that we understand the unique starting points of our learners and what their needs are. The SEND Code of Practice (2015) describes four broad areas of need. These are:

❖ Cognition and Learning.
❖ Communication and Interaction.
❖ Social, Emotional and Mental Health.
❖ Physical and/or Sensory.

We will be exploring these areas in more detail in the background information for each section of the following self-evaluation tools. With all of this in mind, what follows should help you to identify where your classroom practice is at and how to move it forwards. The sections cover:

❖ Lesson planning.
❖ Supporting pupils with cognition and learning needs.
❖ Supporting pupils with communication and interaction needs.
❖ Supporting pupils with social, emotional and mental health needs.
❖ Supporting pupils with physical and/or sensory needs.

1. Lesson Planning

It can be difficult to quantify and capture what makes an outstanding lesson. Often, I am told that you just know it is. Some teachers describe a feeling – some sort of incredible buzz and flow in the classroom. I would describe this as a lesson in which every pupil is engaged and feels safe, secure and motivated to take a learning risk in order to accomplish something that moves them on from their unique starting point.

To make this happen careful consideration needs to be given to the how, what and why of you are going teach. This needs to take account of what your pupils have done before and where you need them to be by the end of the lesson. This needs to also bring to play all of their previous experiences that have led to their current unique starting point. This can be difficult to achieve when you have a wide spread of abilities and previous experiences, coupled with children who are all at different stages of their development.

It should also be remembered that a lesson plan is not set in stone. It should be adaptive and responsive to the emerging needs of our learners as the lesson progresses. Teachers need to be ready to scaffold, motivate and push harder immediately as a direct result of what we discover in the moment.

SUPPORT MATERIAL

1. Lesson planning

Delving deeper	Where could you look?	Developing	Embedding	Secure	Our evidence – we know this because...
1.1 Lesson intentions/objectives are action-orientated and focus upon the pupils' most significant and critical learning demands.	• Lesson plans. • Previous lesson evaluations and reflections.				
1.2 Previous learning and life experiences are honoured and built upon.	• Lesson plans. • Previous lesson evaluations and reflections.				
1.3 Our planning meets pupils at their unique starting points and explores how to drive them forwards from here.	• Lesson plans. • Previous lesson evaluations and reflections. • Examples of pupils' previous work/learning.				
1.4 Resources are identified. Such resources include what is needed for content and what may be needed to promote engagement, access and independence.	• Lesson plans. • Previous lesson evaluations and reflections.				
1.5 Opportunities for making links to previous learning are explicit.	• Lesson plans. • Previous lesson evaluations and reflections.				
1.6 Opportunities for teacher modelling, guided practice and independent work are identified.					
1.7 Appropriate scaffolds are identified to support identified needs.	• Lesson plans. • Previous lesson evaluations and reflections.				
1.8 There are high expectations for all learners.	• Lesson plans. • Previous lesson evaluations and reflections. • Examples of pupils' previous work/learning.				

2. Supporting Pupils with Cognition and Learning Needs

The SEND Code of Practice 2015 defines cognition and learning needs as:

> Support for learning difficulties may be required when children and young people learn at a slower pace than their peers, even with appropriate differentiation. Learning difficulties cover a wide range of needs, including moderate learning difficulties (MLD), severe learning difficulties (SLD), where children are likely to need support in all areas of the curriculum and associated difficulties with mobility and communication, through to profound and multiple learning difficulties (PMLD), where children are likely to have severe and complex learning difficulties as well as a physical disability or sensory impairment.
>
> *(6.30)*

Usually, these needs can be effectively met in the classroom via high-quality adaptive teaching of what is ordinarily available. It is important that, for these learners, we have high expectations in which we scaffold up.

Often to support cognition and learning needs in the classroom, support for executive functioning is required. Executive functioning can be referred to as the management system of the brain. It is the area of our brain which governs the skills involved in setting goals, planning and executing tasks, then seeing them through to the end. The three main areas of executive function are:

❖ Working memory
❖ Cognitive flexibility (also called flexible thinking)
❖ Inhibitory control (which includes self-control)

This can be in addition to supporting the entry level literacy and numeracy skills required to access the task. To achieve all of this, the following needs careful consideration.

2. Supporting pupils with cognition and learning needs

Delving deeper	Where could you look?	Developing	Embedding	Secure	Our evidence – we know this because. . .
2.1 Pupils with cognition and learning needs are identified and staff take account of these needs when lesson planning.	• Lesson plans. • Pupil produced work. • SEN register.				
2.2 There are high expectations for pupils with cognition and learning needs.	• Lesson plans. • Examples of pupil work.				
2.2 The lesson pace is appropriate – pupils with cognition and learning needs are given appropriate time to complete work and appropriate time to process and respond to information and instructions.	• Lesson observations. • Learning walks. • Pupil produced work.				
2.3 Questions are adapted to take account of pupils' knowledge and understanding.	• Lesson observations. • Learning walks.				
2.4 The cognitive load of tasks is carefully considered and compensatory supports are in place. These may include: voice-recording devices, writing frames and task-slicing tools, worked examples to check against.	• Lesson observations. • Learning walks. • Classroom resource audits.				
2.5 Resources are modified so that they are accessible for a range of abilities matched to the pupils' level of literacy and/or numeracy.	• Lesson observations. • Learning walks. • Classroom resource audits.				

(Continued)

Delving deeper	Where could you look?	Developing	Embedding	Secure	Our evidence – we know this because. . .
2.6 Larger tasks are broken down into smaller steps – task slicing.	• Lesson plans. • Lesson observations. • Learning walks. • Examples of pupil produced work.				
2.7 A range of scaffolds are available matched to the needs of learners. This can include scaffolds that promote accessibility and those that can support independence.	• Lesson plans. • Lesson observations. • Learning walks. • Examples of pupil produced work.				
2.8 When needed pupils are given time to revisit concepts and/or carry out additional rehearsal of skills.	• Lesson plans. • Lesson observations. • Learning walks. • Examples of pupil produced work.				
2.9 Curriculum coverage may be modified to prioritise the pupils' most pressing needs.	• Lesson plans. • Lesson observations. • Learning walks. • Examples of pupil produced work.				
2.10 A range of ways for capturing learning are available so that assessment of pupils' knowledge, understanding and skills is not reliant just on written output.	• Lesson plans. • Lesson observations. • Learning walks. • Examples of pupil produced work.				
2.11 Consideration is given as to how the pupils will be taught to remember and retrieve learning.	• Lesson plans. • Lesson observations. • Learning walks. • Examples of pupil produced work.				

3. Supporting Pupils with Communication and Interaction Needs

The SEND Code of Practice 2015 defines communication and interaction needs as:

> Children and young people with speech, language and communication needs (SLCN) have difficulty in communicating with others. This may be because they have difficulty saying what they want to, understanding what is being said to them or they do not understand or use social rules of communication. The profile for every child with SLCN is different and their needs may change over time. They may have difficulty with one, some or all of the different aspects of speech, language or social communication at different times of their lives.

(6.28)

It goes on to note that children and young autistic people are:

> . . . likely to have particular difficulties with social interaction. They may also experience difficulties with language, communication and imagination, which can impact on how they relate to others.

(6.30)

Pupils with communication and interaction needs may have difficulties with developing all or some of the following skills:

❖ Attention and listening: these are active processes. Paying attention and listening involves concentrating on an activity and integrating information from a range of differing sources (such as what you see and what you hear).
❖ Speech production: the process of articulating sounds and words.
❖ Receptive language: the ability to understand and comprehend the language we hear or read.
❖ Expressive language: the ability to express thoughts, needs, feelings and ideas.
❖ Social language and communication: this refers to the use of verbal (spoken language) and nonverbal (eye gaze, facial expression, gestures) communication in social situations, to share what you want, express feelings, relate to other people and develop meaningful relationships. This is often referred to as being able to understand and follow the unwritten rules of social situations.

Having difficulties in this area can inhibit access to learning in the following ways:

- ❖ Understanding the language of teaching.
- ❖ Communicating wants, needs, ideas, opinions and feelings.
- ❖ Following instructions.
- ❖ Task completion.
- ❖ Keeping up with the social demands of the classroom.
- ❖ Making and maintaining friendships.
- ❖ Partner and group work.
- ❖ Demonstrating what you have learnt.

The following self-evaluation tool will help you to identify how the needs of pupils with communication and interaction needs are currently met and what to do in order to move this forward.

3. Supporting pupils with communication and interaction needs

Delving deeper	Where could you look?	Developing	Embedding	Secure	Our evidence – we know this because. . .
3.1 Pupils with communication and interaction needs are identified and staff take account of these needs when lesson planning.	• Lesson plans. • Pupil-produced work. • SEN register.				
3.2 There are high expectations for pupils with communication and interaction needs.	• Lesson plans. • Examples of pupil work.				
3.2 The lesson pace is appropriate – pupils with communication and interaction needs are given appropriate time to complete work and appropriate time to process and respond to information and instructions.	• Lesson observations. • Learning walks. • Pupil voice activities.				
3.3 Subject-specific vocabulary is pre-taught to those that require it.	• Lesson observations. • Learning walks. • Intervention logs.				
3.4 Subject-specific vocabulary is supported with visual cues and/or objects of reference.	• Lesson observations. • Learning walks.				
3.5 Instructions are: • Issued one at a time. • Correctly sequenced. • Personalised where needed. • Supported with visual cues. • Modelled. • Repeated. Learners are given additional processing time where needed.	• Lesson observations. • Learning walks.				
3.6 Strategies are in place to support learners who find it difficult to maintain their attention and listening skills.	• Lesson plans. • Learning walks. • Lesson observations.				

(Continued)

Delving deeper	Where could you look?	Developing	Embedding	Secure	Our evidence – we know this because...
3.7 Background noise is limited to allow pupils to focus upon communication.	• Learning walks, • Lesson observations. • Environmental audits.				
3.8 Signing and/or natural gesture is used to support communication.	• Learning walks. • Lesson observations.				
3.9 Pupils are given opportunities to show as opposed to tell.	• Learning walks. • Lesson observations.				
3.10 Paired talk opportunities are in place so that pupils can rehearse answers before sharing to a wider audience.	• Learning walks. • Lesson observations.				
3.11 Implicit social rules are explained.	• Learning walks. • Lesson observations.				
3.12 Clear rules and roles for partner and/ or group work are shared.	• Learning walks. • Lesson observations.				
3.13 Sentence starters and models are modelled and shared.	• Learning walks. • Lesson observations.				
3.14 Where appropriate strategies and approaches from speech and language therapists/related professionals are incorporated in classroom practice.	• Learning walks. • Lesson observations. • Lesson plans. • Reports from professionals.				

4. Supporting Pupils with Social, Emotional and Mental Health Needs

Prior to the inclusion of social, emotional and mental health needs, children's difficulties in this area were often categorised as coming under emotional and behavioural needs. The change to social, emotional and mental health reflects the fact that behaviour is now perceived as a form of communication which reflects the child's state of mind. This could be caused by a variety of factors such as:

- ❖ Anxiety.
- ❖ Unmet sensory needs.
- ❖ Anger, including anger about pervasive life situations or undisclosed difficulties.
- ❖ A response to socio-economic challenges.
- ❖ A response to trauma or attachment difficulties.
- ❖ Frustration due to unidentified and/or unmet speech and communication difficulties or learning needs.
- ❖ A response to the wrong level of challenge in lessons.
- ❖ Grief.
- ❖ Basic needs not being met such as those relating to hunger.
- ❖ Physical pain or discomfort.
- ❖ Underlying mental health problems.
- ❖ Undisclosed physical, mental or sexual abuse.

This list is illustrative, not exhaustive.

The SEND Code of Practice 2015 defines social, emotional and mental health needs as:

> Children and young people may experience a wide range of social and emotional difficulties which manifest themselves in many ways. These may include becoming withdrawn or isolated, as well as displaying challenging, disruptive or disturbing behaviour. These behaviours may reflect underlying mental health difficulties such as anxiety or depression, self-harming, substance misuse, eating disorders or physical symptoms that are medically unexplained. Other children and young people may have disorders such as attention deficit disorder, attention deficit hyperactive disorder or attachment disorder.

(6.32)

According to the World Health Organisation (2022), mental health is defined as 'a state of well-being in which every individual realises his or her own potential, can cope with the normal stresses of life, can work productively and fruitfully, and is able to make a contribution to her or his community'.

It could be argued that schools are the perfect setting for supporting positive mental health. They play a crucial part in raising awareness, promoting acceptance, reducing stigma and supporting pupils with mental health issues. By providing mentally healthy classrooms, we are able to proactively support positive mental health and wellbeing before challenges arise and give pupils the skills to manage whatever life throws at them.

As discussed earlier when considering 'the feeling', a crucial underpinning of a mental health is a relational approach where there is trust, nurture, acceptance, awareness and a mutual respect. One that acknowledges that everyone is valued for who they are in a totally safe space. In these conditions pupils can foster the positive social, emotional and mental health needed to be resilient, secure risk-taking learners.

4. Supporting pupils with social, emotional and mental health needs

Delving deeper	Where could you look?	Developing	Embedding	Secure	Our evidence – we know this because. . .
4.1 Pupils with social, emotional and mental health needs are identified and staff take account of these needs when lesson planning.	• Lesson plans. • Pupil produced work. • SEN register.				
4.2 There are high expectations for pupils with social, emotional and mental health needs.	• Lesson plans. • Examples of pupil work.				
4.3 A sense of belonging is fostered.	• Pupil voice activities. • Learning walks. • Lesson observations.				
4.4 There are opportunities for pupils to share their worries, feelings and concerns.	• Pupil voice activities. • Learning walks. • Lesson observations. • Environmental audits.				
4.5 The classroom offers a safe space to learn and take risks.	• Pupil voice activities. • Learning walks. • Lesson observations. • Environmental audits.				
4.6 Mistakes are valued as opportunities to learn.	• Pupil voice activities. • Learning walks. • Lesson observations. • Examples of pupil work.				
4.7 Pupils are actively encouraged to share their feelings and how they cope. A range of supportive mechanisms are in place to support the communication of this.	• Pupil voice activities. • Learning walks. • Lesson observations. • Examples of pupil work.				
4.8 Safe spaces and resources to self-regulate are available.	• Pupil voice activities. • Learning walks. • Lesson observations. • Environmental audits.				

(Continued)

Delving deeper	Where could you look?	Developing	Embedding	Secure	Our evidence – we know this because . . .
4.9 The unique skills, talents and strengths of pupils are recognised and celebrated.	• Pupil voice activities. • Learning walks. • Lesson observations.				
4.10 Opportunities (incidental and planned) to teach about mental health and well-being are exploited.	• Learning walks. • Lesson observations. • Examples of pupil produced work.				
4.11 Teachers and support staff are professionally curious about the mental health and well-being of pupils.	• Learning walks. • Lesson observations.				
4.12 Positive relationships between peers and adults and peers are fostered.	• Learning walks. • Lesson observations. • Pupil and staff voice activities.				
4.13 Teachers and support staff know who to approach if they have a concern about a pupil's mental health.	• Staff voice activities.				

5. Supporting Pupils with Physical and/or Sensory Needs

The SEND Code of Practice defines physical and/or sensory needs as:

> Some children and young people require special educational provision because they have a disability which prevents or hinders them from making use of the educational facilities generally provided. These difficulties can be age related and may fluctuate over time. Many children and young people with vision impairment (VI), hearing impairment (HI) or a multi-sensory impairment (MSI) will require specialist support and/or equipment to access their learning, or habilitation support. Children and young people with an MSI have a combination of vision and hearing difficulties. Information on how to provide services for deafblind children and young people is available through the Social Care for Deafblind Children and Adults guidance published by the Department of Health (see the References section under Chapter 6 for a link).

(6.34)

The impact of physical and/or sensory difficulties may be hidden, mild or profound. With the right support and professional knowledge, pupils with these needs can achieve just as much as other pupils.

Section 100 of the Children and Families Act 2014 places a duty on governing bodies of maintained schools, proprietors of academies and management committees of Pupil Referral Units (PRUs) to make arrangements for supporting pupils at their school with medical conditions. Many pupils will be able to successfully participate in all aspects of learning and wider school life. But, for some, their needs may affect their ability to access and engage in learning tasks and activities. Therefore, support may be required through individualised, effective high-quality adaptive teaching that is more than what is ordinarily available and additional interventions.

Sensory impairment (relating to hearing and vision) can have a significant impact on a pupil's educational development and wellbeing, in some cases resulting in learning delays and/or reduced access to learning.

The Children's and Families Act (2014) refers to children and young people either having a learning difficulty or having a disability. In this context a disability means being disabled within the meaning of the Equality Act 2010.

Section 6(1) of the Equality Act 2010 states that:

> A person has a disability if (a) The person has a physical or mental impairment, and (b) the impairment has a substantial and long-term adverse effect on the person's ability to carry out normal day-to-day activities.

Children and young people may be disabled or have a learning difficulty or both. They may or may not need special education provision.

All schools have duties under the Equality Act 2010 towards individual disabled children and young people. They must make reasonable adjustments, including the provision of auxiliary aids and services for disabled children, to prevent them being put at a substantial disadvantage. These duties are anticipatory – they require thought to be given in advance to what disabled children and young people might require and what adjustments might need to be made to prevent that disadvantage. Schools also have wider duties to prevent discrimination, to promote equality of opportunity and to foster good relations.

It is important to note that, as stated in the SEND Code of Practice (2015):

> A pupil has SEN where their learning difficulty or disability calls for special educational provision, namely provision different from or additional to that normally available to pupils of the same age. Making higher-quality teaching normally available to the whole class is likely to mean that fewer pupils will require such support. Such improvements in whole class provision tend to be more cost effective and sustainable.

> (6.15)

Consequently, the impact of a pupil's needs in this area needs to be carefully monitored to decide whether the pupil has SEN, a disability or both.

In addition to the following self-evaluation tool, links should be drawn to the findings from the 'Supporting Pupils with Hearing and/or Vision Impairments' tool in the previous section.

5. Supporting pupils with physical and/or sensory needs

Delving deeper	Where could you look?	Developing	Embedding	Secure	Our evidence – we know this because. . .
5.1 Pupils with physical and/or sensory needs are identified and staff take account of these needs when lesson planning.	• Lesson plans. • Pupil produced work. • SEN register.				
5.2 There are high expectations for pupils with physical and/or sensory needs.	• Lesson plans. • Examples of pupil work.				
5.3 The impact of physical and/or sensory needs and potential fatigue is catered for at the planning stage of lessons.	• Lesson plans.				
5.4 Adapted tools and aids are provided to promote independent access to tasks.	• Lesson plans. • Resource audits. • Examples of pupil produced work.				
5.5 Additional time is offered for the completion of tasks.	• Lesson plans. • Lesson observations. • Learning walks.				
5.6 Seating arrangements are flexible in lessons to meet physical and/or sensory needs.	• Learning walks. • Lesson observations.				
5.7 Alternatives for writing are available.	• Examples of pupil produced work. • Lesson plans.				
5.8 Technology is used to enhance learning resources and increase accessibility.	• Learning walks, • Lesson observations. • Lesson plans.				
5.9 Table-top copies of display resources are available for those that need it. These take account of the pupil's specific needs.	• Learning walks. • Lesson observations.				

(Continued)

Delving deeper	Where could you look?	Developing	Embedding	Secure	Our evidence – we know this because. . .
5.10 Pupils are given opportunities to handle and preview resources prior to classroom learning.	• Lesson plans. • Intervention records.				
5.11 Alternative backgrounds, papers and contrasts are available for reprographics.	• Lesson observations. • Learning walks. • Examples of pupil produced work.				
5.12 Worksheets and recoding formats are enlarged for pupils with motor difficulties to increase the space that they have available to work in.	• Examples of pupil produced work. • Lesson plans.				
5.13 Teachers and support staff take account of the recommendations made by supporting professionals.	• Learning walks. • Lesson observations. • Professional reports.				
5.14 Individual modifications are made to meet needs such as enlarging texts, using a particular font style and offering specific tools.	• Learning walks. • Lesson observations. • Pupil assessments. • Professional reports.				
5.15 Furniture is adaptable and/or matched according to the pupil's physical and/or sensory needs and is used flexibly in lessons.	• Environmental audits. • Lesson plans. • Lesson observations.				

Section Three
THE TOOLKIT

1. Lesson Planning

Every school has its own format for lesson planning. There are no one- size-fits-all methods or templates. However, there are many prompts that can be used to support the thinking processes behind our planning and the pedagogy choices that we make. These prompts can also guide us towards making more conscious and considered resource and approach choices.

What follows is a menu of different strategies and supportive resources that can be deployed in a lesson as part of what is ordinarily available to support and promote greater pupil independence and engagement. The tool is organised into the four broad areas of need as identified in the SEND Code of Practice (2015). Once the learning intention and classroom activities have been decided, teachers can choose from the menu, highlight their selections and deploy in their lessons.

The strategies and resources included are more general and not exhaustive – more of a useful starting point. You can add your own ideas to them. It could also be possible for subject specialists/leaders to create their own for their area. What is included will provide vital support for many learners with additional needs but should be offered to all as an inclusive approach as everyone will benefit!

Additional Support Menu

Learning Intention:				
	Cognition and Learning	*Communication and Interaction*	*Social, Emotional and Mental Health*	*Physical and/or Sensory*
Resources	• Voice-recording device to support with 'holding' information. • Visual timeline as part of a task-slicing approach. • Mini dry-wipe board for jottings. • Timer for task organisation. • Concrete apparatus. • 100 square. • Number line. • Spelling choice chart. • Word mat with added visuals to support spelling and understanding. • Spelling dictionary. • Picture dictionary. • Graphic organisers.	• Voice-recording device containing simplified language for instructions. • Visual timeline. • Now/next board. • Word mat with additional visuals to aid understanding and recall of subject specific vocabulary. • Objects of reference to support key vocabulary. • Access to a low arousal space. • Prompts for group work roles. • Positive prompts for behaviours for learning linked to pragmatic skills.	• Visual timelines to promote routine and security. • Access to a low arousal space. • Sensory tools to aid self-regulation. • Support for transition: prior warning, a countdown with a visual timer, now/next board, objects of reference. • Feelings vocabulary checklists with additional visual supports. • Personalised self-monitoring and regulation charts. • Time-out card. • Comfort objects.	• Writing slope. • Pencil grip. • Adapted tools. • Seating wedge. • Non-slip matting. • Wobble cushion. • Access to Theraputty. • Enlarged resources. • Limiting background noise. • Access to a low arousal space. • Flexible seating arrangements. • Movement breaks. • Access to assistive technology. • Designated work spaces. • A range of background colours to increase contrast for the presentation of information.

(Continued)

153

Learning Intention:				
	Cognition and Learning	*Communication and Interaction*	*Social, Emotional and Mental Health*	*Physical and/or Sensory*
Teaching and learning strategies	• Additional processing time. • Pre-teaching and/or pre-exposure. • Paired talk opportunities to rehearse, clarify and organise ideas. • Peer tutoring. • Additional worked examples. • A model of what finished looks like. • Additional modelling. • Additional guided practice. • Additional retrieval practice in the plenary. • An 'I do, we do, you do' approach to tasks. • Additional time to complete tasks. • Alternatives to writing for recording modelled and provided.	• Added natural gesture. • Signing. • Reduced language levels. • For instructions – shorter, one at a time, sequenced in order, visually supported, repeated. • Additional processing time. • Paired-talk opportunities to rehearse, clarify and organise ideas. • Provision of sentence starters. • Model answers to check against. • Pre-teaching of subject specific vocabulary.	• Wondering aloud: 'I can see that . . . I wonder if this means that. . .' • Identifying and narrating the positive choices made by others. • Specific, directed praise linked to classroom expectations. • Modelling how to fail and recover well. • Agreeing a discreet 'help needed' signal. • Additional support for or limiting of transitions. • Provision of a range of mechanisms to self-identify how they are feeling. This is responded to by adults.	• Provision of a peer buddy. • An 'I do, we do, you do' approach. • Additional time to complete tasks. • Consideration given to potential fatigue in lessons. • Alternatives to writing are modelled and provided.

Top Tips for Planning a Lesson that Can Include All

❖ Know the unique starting point of your learners. Consider how you will meet them at this point to move them forwards.

❖ Start with the bigger picture. What do you want all of your learners to get out of your lesson? Have high expectations!

❖ Consider how you will make this accessible to all. What scaffolds will be needed? How can you support independence and engagement? Offer them to everyone – all will benefit.

❖ Build in time so that pupils can select and access the resources that they need and know how and when to use them effectively.

- ❖ Make explicit links and give value to what the pupils have experienced and learnt before.
- ❖ Make sure that the resources you wish to include are accessible for all. For example, you could consider: font size, a dyslexia-friendly presentation, enlargement and accessibility according to reading skill level.
- ❖ Include as many multi-sensory and hands-on learning opportunities as possible.
- ❖ Consider how the pupils will record their work. Does it have to be written in sentences or could a mind map, diagram, table or picture work equally as well?
- ❖ Look carefully at the resources you provide are the images used and implicit messages given relevant to and representative of your school community.
- ❖ Give specific time for pupils to embed and apply their new learning.
- ❖ Have a hook such as an image, a video, a discussion point, a story, a mystery object, etc. Whatever you choose, use it to engage the children's imagination from the start.
- ❖ Include pupil voice.
- ❖ Include opportunities for discussions and questions.
- ❖ Give pupils choices about the resources they will use, the method they will use and how they will present their work.

2. Supporting Pupils with Cognition and Learning Needs

To support you in meeting some of the more common difficulties that I regularly come across in the classroom linked to cognition and learning, I have created a tool which explores the difficulty and suggests some simple but impactful strategies and the reasons why they can help. It is not an exhaustive list. This tool can be shared with your colleagues as a toolkit from which they can select what they think will work well for them to support their pupils' learning.

Cognition and Learning
Area of difficulty: Memory – The ability to recall consistently what has previously been taught.

What might this difficulty look like in the classroom?
• Inconsistent recall of learning that may vary daily. • A high level of task abandonment. • Difficulties with demonstrating age and ability appropriate task organisation, maintenance and completion skills. • Partially completed instructions. • Requiring considerable time to 'think' and process before answering questions, processing information or following instructions. • Checking against peers for reassurance about what to do and then following. • Looking for visual models in the environment to check against. • Difficulties with word finding. • Frequently losing things or finding it challenging to organise resources. • Common tasks are completed in a random order/sequence. • Difficulties with recalling and following procedures. • Their work is often unrelated to the teacher input. • Needing significantly high levels of repetition. • Appearing distracted. • Difficulties with copying. • Difficulties with place-keeping within a task. • Shares thoughts, needs, wants and opinions immediately.

Suggested Strategies and Resources	How They Can Help
Additional retrieval practice in lessons.	Offers additional time to create traces of what has been taught to make recall easier in the longer term.
Placing key content for recall at the start and the end of learning.	This allows learning to be processed and make the transfer from the short-term memory into the longer-term memory.
Strategies to avoid cognitive overload such as use of a voice recording device to 'hold' information, visual timeline, model of finished to check against, worked examples, respite/refresh breaks, pre-exposure to new materials/resources, eliminate all unnecessary information, make explicit connections to previous learning.	This allows the learner to focus upon content as opposed to process which frees up more memory space.
Pre-teaching and/or pre-exposure to learning resources/material prior to the lesson.	It is easier to recall and engage with familiar material.
Multi-sensory learning opportunities (using more than one sense to interact with and learn new material).	The more modalities we use, the more likely we are to remember.
Increase visual support.	Spoken words disappear but a written record support with high-quality visual supports limit memory demands.

(Continued)

Limit copying – provide a table-top copy of information to work from.	This lessens memory demands as the pupil does not have to hold and transfer information which can slow down output.
Allow time for elaboration processing to make a personalised link that connects new learning with old learning.	We are more likely to remember things that are personally more significant to us.

Area of difficulty: Executive functioning – A set of skills that underlie our capacity to plan ahead and meet goals, display self-control, follow multiple-step directions even when interrupted and stay focused despite distractions, among others.

What might this difficulty look like in the classroom?
- Finding it challenging to select resources for learning with independence.
- Appearing anxious when preparing for a new activity or when asked to 'get ready' for learning.
- Difficulties with organising resources for learning independently.
- Difficulty with sequencing and planning events.
- Often loses possessions.
- Appears to be untidy.
- Frequent task abandonment.
- Finding it challenging to manage their own time and meeting a deadline.
- Difficulties with task execution.
- Difficulties with changing task.
- Work produced is not related to the learning intention.
- Can appear to be distracted.
- Appears to be one step behind what is happening.
- Can become overloaded quickly.

Suggested Strategies and Resources	How They Can Help
Provide a visual equipment checklist.	The pupil will know what is needed so will be able to focus more upon the task in hand.
Ensure that all resources are labelled with words and visual support.	The pupil will be able to find what they need quickly and efficiently.
Increase support for breaking a larger task into smaller steps towards completion. A now/next board, visual timeline, check or 'to-do' list or a colour coded activity timetable can help.	Pupils will be able to focus upon one mini task at a time rather than getting lost in the bigger picture. They will achieve lots of mini successes along the way.
Use of a visual timer device matched to appropriate productivity targets.	This will support time management so that the pupil can complete their work within a given deadline.
Offer respite/refocus breaks.	The pupil will be able to sustain working for longer.
Provide a worked examples and a model of what finished looks like.	This will help the pupil to focus upon what they should be producing so that their output remains relevant to the task.

Area of difficulty: Concentration – The action of focusing attention to see a task through to completion.

What might this look like in the classroom?
- Appears distracted.
- Difficulties with task maintenance.
- Difficulty sustaining attention in an adult-led activity and when working independently.
- Seeks movement opportunities.
- Works in short bursts.
- Flits from task to task.
- Can distract others.
- Displays a higher level of task abandonment compared to peers.
- Struggles to change task independently.
- Partially follows instructions.

(Continued)

- Work produced is not fully linked to tasks.
- Requires a high level of prompting to remain focused.

Suggested Strategies and Resources	How They Can Help
Offer a range of sensory resources that the pupil can use to achieve an appropriate level of self-regulation for learning. These resources should be individually selected to help the pupil: become more alert, remain focused or become calmer. This approach could form part of a wider sensory diet.	If our sensory needs are met, we feel regulated so are more available for learning.
Offer a visual timeline as part of a task-slicing approach. Breaks can be built in to refresh/refocus between tasks.	By breaking down larger tasks into smaller mini-steps pupils are able to work in short bursts but for longer. The feeling of success attached to the completion of each task will promote on-going engagement.
Keep focused tasks short, varied and as multi-sensory and hands on as possible. Work should be interspersed with short, pupil-selected activities.	Pupils are more likely to sustain engagement if tasks are short and feel like fun. They will also be motivated by self-directed approaches.

Area of difficulty: Applying learning – Using what has previously been learnt in novel situations.

What might this look like in the classroom?
- Needs all learning to be presented in exactly the same way and in exactly the same context.
- Experiences difficulties with recognising and applying related facts (such as 3 + 6 = 9 so 30 + 60 = 90).
- Does not easily link learning to previous experiences and/or teaching.
- Relies on learning by rote so lacks conceptual understanding.

Suggested Strategies and Resources	How They Can Help
Present an overview of a task/end product – 'the bigger picture' – and then show how each learning experience contributes to this. This could be presented as a journey to an end goal.	This will make learning links explicit so that pupils can see how things fit together.
Create a visual support that the pupil can see/hold have this out for each linked task so that the pupil can see how the learning applies to the new scenario.	This will make learning links explicit so that pupils can see how things fit together.

Area of difficulty: Entry-level literacy skills – having the pre-requisite literacy skills needed to access learning.

What might this look like in the classroom?
- Difficulties with making the correct phonic choice for accurate reading and/or spelling at a whole word level.
- Difficulties with sequencing sounds.
- Difficulties with phonological processing (for example identifying alliteration, rhyming strings and holding/manipulating sounds).
- Errors are not usually phonetically plausible.
- Limited range/deployment of supportive decoding and encoding strategies or over-reliance on one particular strategy.
- Chooses simpler word choices to avoid spelling particular words.
- Masks spelling errors with illegible handwriting.
- Difficulties with identifying syllables.
- Reluctance to read/write.
- A high level of effort required to read and spell accurately at a whole word level in comparison to their peers.
- Difficulties with making meaning due to the effort load of decoding.
- Unable to express personal opinions about a text.
- Slow reading rate due to the effort load of decoding.
- Inaccurate word recognition.
- Difficulties with tracking (left to right).

(Continued)

- Difficulties with making a return sweep (moving from the end of one line of text to the next line).
- Comprehension of text impacted upon due to losing meaning as the reading is at a slow pace.
- Difficulties with organising written work.
- No or incorrect use of punctuation linked to age-related expectations.

Suggested Strategies and Resources	How They Can Help
Have a range of dictionaries available matched to ability and developmental level. Choices for this can include: picture dictionaries, ACE-spelling dictionaries, personalised dictionaries made for/by individual pupils and electronic devices. Make sure pupils know where to find these and how to use them effectively.	Pupils will have a support tool that they can independently access as required.
Provide table-top spelling strategies, decoding strategies and phonic choices prompt cards to remind pupils of the varying approaches and choices that they could try before seeking support.	This will increase independence and empower pupils to try a self-help strategy first.
Give the pupil a choice of two words to select the correct spelling or word to read from.	This will limit choice, making cognitive overload less likely to occur.
Provide personalised spelling dictionaries and allow pupils to develop and collect their own recall tools such as visual cues and mnemonics to add to these.	We are more likely to connect with and remember what is personally significant to us.
Pre-teach 'tricky' words prior to the lesson.	This will allow pupils to read and write with a greater pace as their spelling/reading when meeting these words will be more automatic.
Model thinking aloud to make the invisible visible whilst modelling reading and writing so that pupils can 'hear' which strategy you have used and why.	Some pupils do not automatically learn strategies and apply them. This approach provides a direct model for them to work from.
Highlight the keyword in the question and the key word/information in the text to support the pupil in making links.	This will help the pupil navigate texts efficiently and locate the information that they need to make meaning.
Encourage the pupil to reproduce the information that they have read in an alternative format such as a table, mind map or diagram to encourage processing.	This will encourage the pupil to interact with the information provided and process it in order to make meaning.
Use of graphic organisers (such as a writing frame) for writing.	Writing frames will help pupils to recall, organise and record their intentions for writing.
As a writing planning tool – write one idea per post-it note and move around to sequence, 'bin' all ideas that are not needed.	This approach will support the organisation of writing and limit cognitive load as one idea can be focused upon at a time.
Use of a voice-recording device.	This resource can be used for a pupil to record the sentence that they wish to record. They can play back and check content as they record as many times as needed.

3. Supporting Pupils with Communication and Interaction Needs

To support you in meeting some of the more common difficulties that I regularly come across in the classroom linked to communication and interaction, I have created a tool which explores the difficulty, suggests some simple but impactful strategies and the reasons why they can help. It is not an exhaustive list. This tool can be shared with your colleagues as a toolkit from which they can select what they think will work well for them in supporting their pupils.

Communication and Interaction	
Area of difficulty: Pragmatic skills – understanding and applying the unspoken and unwritten skills of communication in social situations.	
What might this difficulty look like in the classroom?	
<ul><li>Displays difficulties with understanding and applying the unspoken rules of social communication at an age- appropriate level.</li><li>Does not recognise and respond to the needs of the listener consistently.</li><li>Over-shares information or easily deviates from the topic of conversation.</li><li>Difficulties with accessing or sustaining group work with peers.</li><li>Does not recognise the personal space of others or have their own personal space.</li><li>Difficulties with taking turns and maintaining turn taking in a conversation.</li><li>Can appear rude or lack a filter but this is usually unintentional.</li><li>Makes too much or too little eye contact.</li><li>Misreads situations so does not give a 'typical' social response.</li><li>Difficulties with interpreting and then responding to body language and facial expressions.</li><li>Talking with the appropriate intonation, speed and volume.</li><li>Interpreting what the speaker intended (implicit messages), not just interpreting the words at a literal level. For example: 'it's dark in here', meaning turn on the light.</li><li>Matching their response to the emotion of the other person.</li></ul>	
Suggested Strategies and Resources	*How They Can Help*
Develop 'good talking' and 'good listening' prompt cards containing visuals to support the development of specific target skills. These cards should make explicit the behaviours that underlie these prompts.	Pupils will know exactly what is required of them – making the implicit, explicit.
Mark space boundaries on tables with masking tape.	This will help pupils to judge the space that they and others have.
Always give a clear role/purpose in group work. Provide a brief checklist of what that role looks like/involves.	This will support the pupil to know exactly what is expected of them in the role that has been given.
Teach inference skills explicitly in context. 'It is hot in here. What might that mean I need you to do to help?'	Pupils will learn typical responses to implicit information and act upon this.
Avoid indirect/implicit instructions such as: 'Can you give out the scissors, please?' A more effective instruction would be: 'Please give one pair of scissors to each person on your table.'	A direct question will help pupils to know precisely what is expected of them and then act accordingly.

(Continued)

Identify what the other pupils are doing and why that might be happening to develop situational understanding. 'I can see that Usman is sitting all by himself at that table. I wonder if he has got no one to work with.' This could be developed to then include teaching about what could be done to react appropriately to the situation.	This will help the pupil to link what is happening to what is needed so will improve their social comprehension.

Area of difficulty: Receptive and expressive language development – receptive language is the words that are understood. Expressive language is the words that are used.

What might this difficulty look like in the classroom?

- Finding it difficult to understand vocabulary.
- Using the 'wrong' word.
- Finding it difficult to use the correct word in the correct context because of lack of understanding.
- Difficulties with following instructions.
- Finds storing and retrieving vocabulary difficult.
- Often the last to follow an instruction; perhaps checks what peers are doing first.
- Uses non-specific vocabulary such as 'thingie'.
- Over-uses natural gesture to support verbal communication.
- Does not always understand jokes.
- Difficulties with making semantic links (knowing what links together such as: knife, fork and spoon – cutlery.)
- Using very limited language, perhaps only making their immediate needs known, rather than commenting or enquiring.

Suggested Strategies and Resources	How They Can Help
Pre-teaching of subject-specific vocabulary.	This will increase pupils' engagement as they will know what the words mean in advance of the lesson.
Make vocabulary mats available as a table-top resource with supporting visuals.	Pupils will be able to have independent access to a resource which will support their understanding of meaning.
Agree a discreet signal for the learner to show when they have not understood.	This avoids potential embarrassment.
Provide the pupil with a personal connection to the information – something that resonates with them.	We are more likely to understand and use information that has a personal connection.
Provide visual cues for key question words.	Pupils will know what sort of answer is required from the question word.

4. Supporting Pupils with Social, Emotional and Mental Health Needs

To support you in meeting some of the more common difficulties that I regularly come across in the classroom linked to social, emotional and mental health needs, I have created a tool which explores the difficulty, suggests some simple but impactful strategies and the reasons why they can help. It is not an exhaustive list. This tool can be shared with your colleagues as a toolkit from which they can select what they think will work well for them.

Social, Emotional and Mental Health	
Area of difficulty: Self-monitoring and regulation skills – the ability to identify how you are feeling and self-manage these emotions to reach a state of regulation.	
What might this difficulty look like in the classroom? • Finding it difficult to recognise and manage their own emotions. • Disproportionate responses to situations. • Difficulties with identifying and responding to emotions of others. • Changes in mood that can be extreme, unpredictable and/or very quick.	
Suggested Strategies and Resources	*How They Can Help*
Regularly review how a pupil's body is feeling; connect this to an emotion and what the pupil might do in terms of actions and behaviours to manage this emotion. This will then lead to 'how can I help myself' and 'how can others help me'. It is important children learn that each emotion is natural, and we all feel them; however, our reactions and behaviours when we feel emotions may result in negative consequences.	Pupils will begin to connect their physiology to their emotional state and act accordingly in a more proportionate manner.
Introduce a self-soothing breathing activity – teach this explicitly and use when the pupil appears to become dysregulated.	Pupils will have an independent self-regulation tool which they can use in learning situations as needed.
Offer a classroom safe space for withdrawal. Ideally, this should be a low arousal area. Agree how long the pupil can remain there and what sort of activities are acceptable. A pop-up tent may provide a helpful self-regulation space.	Having a low arousal safe space limits the extraneous factors that pupils will have to filter. This will aid them to self-regulate and become available for learning.
Area of difficulty: Self-esteem – how we value and perceive ourselves. It's based on our opinions and beliefs about ourselves.	
What might this difficulty look like in the classroom? • Finds it challenging to accept a compliment/accept praise. • Can be overly critical of themselves. • Lacks appropriate assertiveness and the capacity to make decisions. • Can be reluctant to try new things as is scared to risk failure. • Does not believe that they are good enough. • Exhibits disproportionate self-blame. • Finds it difficult to identify own strengths and positive attributes. • Places undue pressure on themselves. • Lacks confidence. • Does not recognise that they deserve happiness.	

(Continued)

Suggested Strategies and Resources	How They Can Help
Support the pupil to develop a personalised daily diary of accomplishments in lessons. They could share this with a trusted adult/peer.	The pupil will gradually learn to identify their own positives as this becomes a routine. This will lead them to look out and celebrate their own achievements.
To begin with offer small, private praise.	They may respond better to less public displays of their strengths and begin to find this easier to accept over time.
When beginning a new learning activity/approach support the pupil to identify the skills and strengths that they already have in place that they can transfer to the task. Work on developing metacognition skills would support this.	The pupil will begin to recognise that they already have many positive characteristics and skills from which they can build.
Offer the pupil positions of responsibility to elevate their status and develop a feeling of self-worth. They may like to support a younger or less able to pupil to complete a task or have responsibility for taking messages to other staff members.	This gives the pupil value and purpose which can raise self-esteem.
Openly acknowledge and model that it is okay to make mistakes. During adult-led activities, role play making a mistake and talk through how to recover.	This demonstrates that we are not all perfect and that making mistakes is perfectly natural.
Demonstrate that the pupil is held in mind: 'I was thinking about you when . . .'	The pupil will know that they are valued.
Ensure that lessons contain the appropriate level of challenge and scaffolding supports and include several opportunities for success. Have clear success criteria so that the pupil will recognise when they have done well. This could take the form of a checklist for the pupil to mark.	Feeling a sense of success and achievement will help the pupil to feel positive about themselves.

Area of difficulty: Developing positive attachments – the relationships and bonds between people.

What might this look like in the classroom?
- Does not seem aware of or to enjoy the company of others and/or does not seek contact with others.
- Displays a limited emotional range.
- Not responding when talked to and/or displaying limited attention.
- Dislikes physical contact with others.
- Does not like direct attention and will avoid social interaction.
- Finds it difficult to build relationships with special people.
- They are not wary of unfamiliar people.
- They are reluctant or show no interest in exploring new situations with support from a familiar adult.
- Limited friendship circle.
- Is reluctant to explore independently even when supported by a familiar adult.
- May present as 'clingy' and anxious.
- Reactions to new situations may be extreme even when with a calm familiar adult.
- Can be determined to work independently and meet their needs on their own.
- Lacking in trust.
- May be high-achieving in some aspects, but are generally socially uncomfortable.
- May be highly vigilant.

Suggested Strategies and Resources	How They Can Help
Within the setting or a specific lesson allocate a consistent key worker or peer to build a relationship with the pupil.	This will help the pupil to build a relationship with a consistent and predictable adult who can then provide a safe base for them to explore and take risks from.

(Continued)

Create spaces and regular opportunities for sustained 1:1 distraction-free interaction. Make these interactions predictable by using familiar toys, games, actions and sounds.	This will offer a safe and predictable structure to learn to build positive interactions and relationships.
Demonstrate that the pupil is held in mind: 'I was thinking about you when . . . '	The pupil will recognise that they matter and are valued. This will encourage them to build positive relationships as they understand that they are wanted by others.
Gently encourage the pupil to seek help from adults and peers.	The pupil will begin to recognise that relationships with others have value.

Area of difficulty: Anxiety – a feeling of unease, such as worry or fear, that can be mild or severe.	
What might this look like in the classroom?	

- Appears uneasy or 'on edge'.
- Can find it difficult to accept and move on from a specific issue and/or theme.
- May be reluctant to try new learning experiences/activities.
- Has irrational or disproportionate fears or phobias.
- Social choices may change.
- Physical symptoms such as feeling ill, getting very hot, headaches.
- Sleep disturbance so presents as more tired than usual.
- Can become fatigued very easily.
- Changes in attendance or school classroom performance.
- Places undue and unrealistic pressure upon themselves.
- Often expects the worst-case scenario as an outcome.

Suggested Strategies and Resources	*How They Can Help*
Work on grading worries and considering the sorts of responses that would be appropriate.	This will help the pupil to recognise their concerns and react in a more disproportionate manner.
Introduce a self-soothing breathing activity such as star breathing. Provide a supporting visual to help the pupil focus.	The pupil will have a self-regulating strategy at their disposal to use when they become anxious.
Use a peer buddy to model new activities and offer pre-teaching to make the unfamiliar feel familiar. Support transitions by offering advance warning, implementing visual support such as a now and next timeline, using a visual timer to show how long and acknowledging that the change may be worrying but support is available.	The familiar feels far more comfortable than the unfamiliar. This may lessen anxiety.
Develop a place for the pupil to note their anxieties so that they can be addressed at an appropriate time.	By sharing their anxieties pupils are less likely to carry them with them and perseverate upon them. They will know that support is available and will be given.

Area of difficulty: Lack of resilience – the capacity to withstand or to recover quickly from difficulties.	
What might this look like in the classroom?	

- Difficulties with responding to perceived challenges or perceived failure.
- Can lack a sense of hope.
- Finds it challenging to adapt to changes.
- 'Gives in' quickly.
- Displays high levels of frustration.
- Places blame on others.
- Can feel helpless and/or hopeless.

(Continued)

Suggested Strategies and Resources	How They Can Help
Develop a structured script to approach problem solving-based tasks: What is the problem? What are all the things I can do to handle it? What will happen if I do each of those things? Which way of handling it is the best? Now that I have tried it, how did I do? Can I do anything differently next time?	Taking the emotion out of the situation and providing a framework will provide a sense of predictability and safety.
Model and celebrate 'failure' and making mistakes as a way of learning that can lead to a positive outcome.	This will normalise failure as part of the learning process and show that it can be a positive outcome. This may make these situations easier to cope with and manage.

Area of difficulty: Self-confidence – a positive feeling about oneself and the world that leads to courageous actions born out of a sense of self-respect.

What might this look like in the classroom?

- Makes limited or no attempt to use voice, gesture, eye contact and facial expression to interact with people and keep their attention.
- Prefers not to seek help.
- Is distressed or reluctant to explore new activities or environments.
- Limited relationships with peer group.
- Over-reliance on adults to and peers to anticipate their needs.
- Can lack independence.

Create activities, spaces and regular opportunities for sustained 1:1 distraction-free interaction in which the pupil can have developing experiences of taking the lead.	The pupil will develop a sense of control and begin to grow their confidence in their own ability to lead.
Identify the skills that the pupil already has in place before tackling a task.	This will support the pupil to recognise that they have existing skills to draw upon and value themselves.
Ensure that all learning activities pose the correct level of challenge and will lead to success.	The feeling of success will develop confidence as the pupil begins to recognise what they can achieve.

5. Supporting Pupils with Physical and/or Sensory Needs

To support you in meeting some of the more common difficulties that I regularly come across in the classroom linked to physical and/or sensory needs I have created a tool which explores the difficulty, suggests some simple but impactful strategies and the reasons why they can help. It is not an exhaustive list. This tool can be shared with your colleagues as a toolkit from which they can select what they think will work well for them in supporting their pupils.

Physical and/or Sensory Needs	
Area of difficulty: Fine motor skills – small muscles working with the brain and nervous system to control movements in areas such as the hands, fingers, lips, tongue and eyes.	
What might this difficulty look like in the classroom?	
• Difficulties with in-hand manipulation of small items. • Difficulties with holding scissors correctly and cutting. • Difficulties with developing a comfortable and effective pen/pencil grip. • General tool skills are not age appropriate. • Difficulties with applying the correct amount of pressure. • Self-care skills such as dressing and eating are challenging to execute independently. • Pencil control is not age appropriate.	
Suggested Strategies and Resources	*How They Can Help*
Offer a range of adapted and progressive tools for all classroom activities such as triangular-grip pencils, easy-grip scissors, rulers with a handle.	Pupils will have the right, accessible tool for the task so will be able to work with greater comfort and control. They may sustain writing for longer.
Offer larger lines/squares to write in.	Pupils will be able to record their work clearly and communicate want they know and understand more effectively.
Offer tools to support the correct posture for writing such as a writing slope and seating wedge.	Pupils will have the correct posture for writing which will increase their comfort levels. This will increase their ability to sustain writing for longer.
Allow additional time for completing fine motor skills-based tasks and allow for potential fatigue.	Engagement with tasks will increase.
Offer alternatives to writing for recording.	Pupils work will reflect what they truly know and understand.
Area of difficulty: Gross motor skills – the skills that children develop using their whole body.	
What might this difficulty look like in the classroom?	
• May exhibit poor core strength – appear floppy. • Difficulties with navigating spaces. • Difficulties with balancing and climbing. • Can present as 'clumsy'.	
Suggested Strategies and Resources	*How They Can Help*
Support posture for table-top activities – resources such as a writing slope and seating wedge can help.	The pupil will be more comfortable so can engage with an activity for longer.
Add natural movement breaks into classroom activities. These could be to punctuate learning as an opportunity to refocus/refresh. Opportunities to move around the room could be built in as a classroom 'job' such as giving out resources.	The breaks will not only develop gross motor skills but will also support comfort levels increasing engagement in activities over time.

(Continued)

Area of difficulty: Sensory processing – a neurological condition in children that can affect the way the brain processes information from the senses.

What might this look like in the classroom?

Visual:

Sensory seeking (hyposensitivity):
- Flapping hands in front of face.
- Concentration on peripheral vision.
- Poor depth perception.
- Fascination with light.

Sensory sensitive (hypersensitive):
- Finds colours, patterns, lights distressing.
- Focus on visual details rather than the big picture.
- Dislikes bright lights.
- Looking down, covering or closing eyes.

Auditory (hearing):

Sensory seeking (hyposensitivity):
- Makes own noises.
- Ignores certain sounds but tunes into others.
- Enjoys noisy places.

Sensory avoiding (hypersensitivity):
- Covers ears in response to sounds.
- Makes own noises.
- Difficulty concentrating.
- Able to hear distant better than close sounds.
- Noise of computers, lights, white boards can be distracting and/or distressing.

Taste:

Sensory seeking (hyposensitivity):
- Eating inappropriate objects and material.
- Liking strong or unusual flavours.

Sensory avoiding (hypersensitivity):
- Fussy eater.
- Liking of bland food.
- Certain textures cause discomfort.

Smell:

Sensory seeking (hyposensitivity):
- Licking objects or people.
- Sniffing objects or people.
- Seeking out strong odours.

Sensory avoiding (hypersensitivity):
- Dislike of particular areas in school based upon smell.
- Dislike of body smells.
- Dislike of breath smells for example coffee residue.

Tactile (touch):

Sensory seeking (hyposensitivity):
- Needing to touch people, objects, and materials – texture seeking.
- Self-harming.
- A high pain threshold.
- Liking pressure, for example: tight clothes and hugs.

Sensory avoiding (hypersensitivity):
- Tactile defensive.

(Continued)

167

- Resistant to physical contact.
- Inability to touch certain substances, textures and/or clothes.
- Resistant to hair and teeth brushing.

Vestibular (balance) and Proprioception (body awareness):
- Rocking, spinning, flapping.
- Bumping into objects and people.
- Being unaware of body position or personal space.
- Touches other pupils when sitting on the carpet, 'can't keep their hands to themselves'.
- May be overly physical with others – unaware of own strength.
- Fear of PE apparatus, reluctance to join in with physical games.
- Poor judgement of depth. For example, difficulties climbing and jumping off apparatus.
- Low muscle tone, floppy, weak, stumbles.
- Leans against walls and furniture, runs hands along the wall when walking down a corridor.
- Likes to jump and lie on the floor.
- Problems manipulating small objects, for example tying shoe laces.
- Movement of whole body to look at something.
- Difficulty with starting and stopping.

Suggested Strategies and Resources	*How They Can Help*
Visual • Adjust lighting to make the child comfortable. • Allow access to a low arousal area that is less visually cluttered. • Offer an individual table/ desk lamp. • Matt surfaces/laminate wallets to reduce glare. • Roller blinds and blackout curtains. • Banish clutter. • Use light to draw attention.	
Auditory (hearing) • Provide ear defenders or a soft headband which can be pulled down over ears. • Use of a personal music player to listen to whilst working or use as a calming strategy. Listen to recordings of natural sounds such as a rainstorm, waves, animals etc. • Use of furniture, cushions, drapes rugs and carpet to absorb noise. • Check for 'buzzing' from electrical equipment and minimise where possible.	By having their sensory needs met pupils are more likely to be able to focus upon learning as they will be in a regulated state.
Taste • Act as a role model and eat alongside the pupil. • Provide choices. Incorporate crunchy, chewy or sticky snacks throughout the day for those that like to chew.	
Smell • Work on desensitisation to smells. Begin with small amounts for short periods of time. • Explore which scents calm or stimulate the pupil. Calming scents are vanilla and rose; peppermint and lemon are usually invigorating. • Replicate home smells at school, e.g. washing powder, air fresheners.	

(Continued)

Tactile (touch) • Provide a small box containing a range of tactile materials such as silk ribbon, various grades of sandpaper, corrugated card, felt, velvet, elastic/ Lycra backed with Velcro so that children can stick them onto their desks to stroke according to their sensory needs – a menu. • Allow the pupil to leave lessons early or late to avoid crowds. • Variations on school uniform: may stipulate colour but style to suit. For example, a scarf instead of a tie, round necks instead of collars, tighter clothing to provide deeper pressure. • Allow clothing not to be tucked in.	
Vestibular • Provide support and reassurance in PE lessons. • Provide a peer buddy to demonstrate movements first so that the pupil can judge speed, force, depth and possible vestibular impact. • Teach self-awareness and monitoring, e.g. 'check-ins', pre-activity talks and reflection activities. • Opportunities for regular, rhythmical bouncing such as use of a therapy ball for seating. • Swinging activities. • Incorporate movement in activities — pass things around a group, put chairs away, collect objects.	
Proprioception • Heavy work activities such as climbing, sweeping, pushing and pulling games. • Indicate boundaries with tape. • Provide a 'sitting spot'. • Use of a peer buddy to model and lead. • Allow leaning against furniture/ walls. • Avoid dangling feet. • Provide a weighted blanket or lap weight.	

Area of difficulty: Hearing and/or vision impairment – reduced hearing and/or vision.	
What might this look like in the classroom? • Hearing and vision impairments can be wide-ranging. It is important to seek advice from specialists about how these difficulties may act as barriers to learning in the classroom. • It is also important to discuss what makes learning more challenging as well as easier to access with the individual pupil and their family.	
Suggested Strategies and Resources	*How They Can Help*
It is important that specialist advice is sought as appropriate. The following are general supportive strategies that may need adapting according to the individual pupil's needs.	
Hearing Impairment • Think carefully about the pupil's seating position. Provide a global view of the classroom so that they have access to lip patterns of all children and staff. For pupils with a unilateral (in one ear) hearing loss ensure their best ear is facing the teacher/ group.	Increased curriculum access, engagement and independence.

(Continued)

• Ensure that the speaker's face is visible and encourage only one person to speak at a time. • Offer pre- and post-teaching sessions focusing upon key vocabulary, instructions and concepts. • Ensure that there is a high level of visual support and identify the specific linked visual at the appropriate time. • Allow enough time for the pupil to look at the visual material before you start talking again – this gives them time to focus their attention back on the teacher or the teaching assistant. • Deploy subtitles when watching a video. Ensure that any additional listening equipment is appropriately connected to the whiteboard. • Provide a note-taker (adult or peer) to record key information from a video as deaf pupils will be unable to make notes at the same time as watching a video. • Be mindful of the level of background noise in the classroom. The pupil should be seated away from sound sources such as fans, computers, radiators and doors. • Improve classroom acoustics and make reasonable adjustments in order to absorb unwanted noise. For example, use of displays, soft furnishings, felt on bottom of pencil pots. • Build additional processing time into lessons, particularly if they contain new information or a 'question and answer' session. • Encourage the pupil to self-advocate by signalling if they cannot hear or have not understood. • Use open-ended questions to check understanding, as this prevents the pupil from nodding without really understanding. • Become familiar with individual signs of tiredness and fatigue.	
Vision Impairment • Plan ahead to make sure you/support staff have time to modify materials before the lesson. Make sure support staff know exactly what is required and by when. • Consider producing materials for all pupils in an accessible font size (at least 14 point) and typeface (e.g. Arial) to reduce the amount of modification needed. • Prepare resources electronically so that they can be saved and modified easily to produce different versions. • Provide additional time, if needed, for pupils with visual impairments to process information and complete tasks. Where extra time is not possible, think about the simplest approach or resource that will enable them to meet the learning outcomes. • Allow for fatigue. • Encourage the pupil to self-advocate and signal if they can't see clearly or make independent adjustments to their seating arrangements or resources.	Increased curriculum access, engagement and independence.

SO WHAT NOW?

Maintenance and Innovation Planning

It is great to have an evidence-based picture of where you are now and where you can go to further develop your inclusive policies, procedures and practices. However, the further developing part can feel a little overwhelming – especially in terms of knowing where to start and what to prioritise. That's where maintenance and innovation planning can be really supportive. I prefer this approach to action planning or development planning as the maintenance aspect gives us the opportunity to recognise and celebrate what is already strong so that we can keep this going. All too often, embedded good practice can slip whilst we pour all of our attention into improving. The innovation is the focus for what will push us forwards.

A solid maintenance and innovation plan will:

❖ Have a 'golden thread' that draws links to your quality assurance work, staff appraisal and your SEN specific values and vision.
❖ Have a clear link to pupil progress, outcomes and engagement.
❖ Be future-focused.
❖ Have limited content so that the focus remains sharp.
❖ Be realistic.
❖ Meets you where you are now.
❖ Reflect sound and honest evaluation.

DOI: 10.4324/9781032643076-8

Here is a potential template:

Area to Develop: Specify if this is a maintenance or an innovation task.					
Target: This needs to be specific, measurable, achievable, realistic and time-bound.					
Task	Who?	Resources and Cost	Timescales and Checkpoints	So What?	Outcome
What will you do to achieve the target? There may be more than one task.	Name the responsible person.	Be precise – if time to complete an action is the resource, provide the cost of this time. This might be, for example, the cost of covering a class teacher for a morning.	Include dates and what success will look like along the way.	What will be different? What will it look like?	What happened as a result?

Here is an example of a completed innovation task.

Area to Develop: Innovation Task Measuring Impact of Interventions					
Target: To evidence transference of learning from withdrawal interventions back into the classroom.					
Task	Who?	Resources and Cost	Timescales and Mini-Milestones	So What?	Outcome
1. Develop the use of link tasks. 2. Introduce evidence gathering books that show how pupils have used their learning from intervention in the classroom.	SENCO will introduce TAs will set link tasks Class teachers will gather relevant evidence.	1. Intervention evidence books cost £100. 2. Special needs leader time – one afternoon. (£250 cover cost) 3. One staff meeting to introduce.	Jan 2023 – link tasks in place, TAs setting the tasks and class teachers completing the evidence books. March 2023 – monitoring of tasks and evidence completed. July 2023 – complete	Pupils explicitly demonstrate their learning from interventions in the classroom. They will have a clear idea of how to use their learning in a real context as evidenced in their evidence books.	Pupil progress accelerated in classrooms. Average SEN pupil progress now in line with non-SEN pupils. Lesson monitoring shows evidence of links made by pupils (see learning walk 3.05.2023).

Finally, I wish you well on your journey of self-evaluation and pushing forwards to meet the needs of your pupils so that they can have the brightest tomorrow.

GLOSSARY

Accessibility The quality of being easy to gain and/or use.

Activities of Daily Living (ADLs) Activities of Daily Living are the essential, basic self-care tasks that need to be completed every day for people to keep themselves safe, healthy, clean and feeling good. Examples include: bathing, grooming, dressing, managing personal care, feeding and travelling.

Aided Language Display (ALD) An Aided Language Display (ALD) is a symbol display on a single page containing relevant symbolised vocabulary for a specific activity.

Children and Families Act 2014 The Children and Families Act 2014 brought together a number of changes to legislation regarding services for vulnerable children and young people and families. The provisions in the Act which relate to special educational needs and disability (SEND) came into force in September 2014.

Co-Production Co-production allows all involved to work collaboratively as equal partners to design, plan, deliver and review support and services in order to achieve shared outcomes. All are recognised as assets that have important contributions to make.

Disability Under the Equality Act 2010 a disability is evident if a person has a physical or mental impairment that has a 'substantial' and 'long-term' negative effect on your ability to do normal daily activities.

Education and Health Care Plan (EHCP) An education, health and care plan is for children and young people up to the age 25 who need more support than is available through special educational needs support. An EHCP identifies the child/young person's educational, health and social needs and sets out the additional support to meet those needs.

Fine Motor Skills Fine motor skills are the ability to make movements using the small muscles in our hands and wrists. We rely on these skills to do key tasks in school, at work and in everyday life such as writing, cutting, measuring, holding and manipulating items.

Formative Assessment Frequent, interactive in-the-moment assessments of student progress and understanding to identify learning needs and adjust teaching appropriately.

Habilitation Involves one-to-one training for children and young people with a vision impairment. Starting from their existing skills, it aims to develop their personal mobility, navigation and independent living skills.

High-Quality Teaching As the fundamental 'bread and butter' of effective learning opportunities, high quality teaching takes account of each pupil's unique starting point. It is responsive and adaptive to the needs of pupils and anticipates and deals with misconceptions to ensure long-term retention of knowledge, fluency in key skills, development of independence and confident use of metacognitive strategies.

Learning Walk A brief visit to each classroom with a key focus in mind that allows school leaders to reflect upon and quality-assure what and how pupils are learning and the environment within which they are working.

Object of Reference A physical object that can be used to represent an activity, a person or a place. Objects of reference stand for something in the same way that words do. They can be used to aid understanding or support those that may find text difficult to access.

Pedagogy The method, and practice of, teaching.

Reasonable Adjustment Reasonable adjustments are changes that organisations and people providing services or public functions have to make if a disability disadvantages a person compared with others who are not disabled. They should be anticipatory.

Responsible Body The governing body or the local authority for maintained schools in England and Wales, the education authority in the case of maintained schools in Scotland, and the proprietor in the case of independent schools, academies or non-maintained special schools.

Sans Serif A style of font that does not contain serifs (the slight projection finishing off a stroke of a letter in particular typefaces).

Seating Wedge Seating wedges are specially shaped cushions that can be used on a chair. The wedge brings a slight downward slope to the seat which positions the user's body into a more comfortable sitting position to alleviate aches and improve posture.

Special Educational Needs (SEN) 'A pupil has SEN where their learning difficulty or disability calls for special educational provision, namely provision different from or additional to that normally available to pupils of the same age.' (6.15 Special Educational Needs and Disability Code of Practice 2015: 0 to 25 years)

Task Slicing A method of breaking large tasks into several small stages. A visual aid can be used to support this.

Visual Timeline A visual timeline is a visual account of a task or a child's routine throughout the day. Each task/lesson is represented by words and pictures, displayed for all to see.

Word Web A type of mind map that can support with learning about new words and expand vocabulary. Word webs help pupils break down the word, understand what it means and make links to other words that they have already learnt.

Writing Slope A sloped platform that can be placed on top of a pupil's desk for them to work on. It encourages users to have a better working posture and wrist position, which helps to improve handwriting.

BIBLIOGRAPHY

Arnstein, S. (1969) A ladder of citizen participation. *Journal of the American Planning Association*, 35(4), 216–224.

Department for Education (2013a) *The Equality Act 2010 and Schools*. Available at: https://www.gov.uk/government/publications/equality-act-2010-advice-for-schools

Department for Education (2013b) *The National Curriculum in England: Key Stages 1 and 2 Framework Document*. Available at: https://www.gov.uk/government/publications/national-curriculum-in-england-primary-curriculum

Department for Education (2015) *SEND Code of Practice: 0 to 25 Years*. Available at: https://www.gov.uk/government/publications/send-code-of-practice-0-to-25

Department for Education (2019) *Early Career Teacher Framework*. Available at: https://assets.publishing.service.gov.uk/media/60795936d3bf7f400b462d74/Early-Career_Framework_April_2021.pdf

Department for Education (2021) *Teachers' Standards*. Available at: https://www.gov.uk/government/publications/teachers-standards

Equality Act (2010) Available at: https://www.legislation.gov.uk/ukpga/2010/15/contents

New Zealand Ministry of Education (1996) *Te Whariki Early Childhood Curriculum*. Wellington: Learning Media Ltd.

Osterman, K. (2000) Students' need for belonging in the school community. *Review of Educational Research*, 70(3), 323–367.

Oxford English Dictionary (2023) 'Ethos, n.' Oxford University Press. Available at https://www.oed.com/search/dictionary/?scope=Entries&q=ethos

World Health Organisation (2022) *Mental Health*. Available at https://www.who.int/news-room/fact-sheets/detail/mental-health-strengthening-our-response